TT

Shane Flynn & Madeline Duffy

Copyright © 2014 Shane Flynn and/or Madeline Duffy

All rights reserved.

ISBN-10: 1500487074
ISBN-13: 978-1500487072

DEDICATION

This work is dedicated to Almighty God

The Father, the Son and the Holy Spirit.

ACKNOWLEDGMENTS

I, Andy Fallon would like to thank all of the Nurses, Doctors, and Health Care Providers, especially those who work in the Intensive Care Units (ICU) at all the hospitals for their knowledge, skill, dedication, perseverance, understanding, compassion and many more adjective's too numerous to mention. Without these people and God Himself to guide them, many of us wouldn't be here today - many thanks to all who were part of this journey and directly contributed to my welfare and well-being.

Thanks to all who contributed and encouraged me to share my story in the form of this book after six years of simply talking with anyone who would listen. To both Shane Flynn, and particularly to Madeline Duffy, for her encouragement, assistance, strength, listening abilities and love which made all of this possible. To Diane Nicholls whose depiction of the cover art is as if she's standing over my shoulder and watching the events unfold.

As I've said, "I'm only the Messenger"…..here's my message…

.

CONTENTS

	Preface	v
1	Back to the beginning	7
2	Caite	49
3	Panic	63
4	The first death	85
5	The fight	95
6	Unplugged?	103
7	The Choice	119
8	Before and after	139
	About the authors	157
	About the artist	159
	Links	161

PREFACE

Between February 6, 2008 and March 12, 2008, Andrew Fannon died twice. This is the true life story leading up to his deaths, what he experienced during his deaths, and his return to this world. He was given a choice. Andy could have chosen to go on or return to this world and fight his way past his divorcing wife. Vicky wants to unplug Andy to get all the assets. Divorce can be an ugly thing, bringing out the worst in people. In the struggle of good vs. evil, does good always win? This is Andy's story of that journey. Is there a supernatural world surrounding us engaged in a battle? Are we the soldiers engaged in that battle? These are questions presented in this book. An eye witness account of the afterlife that you will never forget. Would you have chosen the same way? Are there hidden messages throughout life that we fail to recognize? Is God actually talking to us through familiar events, sounds and signs?

Some of these questions will go unanswered. You'll have to decide your own answers. But perhaps it will make you more aware of the seemingly innocent events that surround your everyday life. Is that smell supposed to remind you of something? Is that sign supposed to give you a message? Some people call it déjà vu. It might be that familiar event that pops into your life for no real reason or something that you remember from somewhere. Is God or an angel trying to communicate something to you by using something in your memory, something familiar?

We've known Andy for many years and totally believe his experience was real. Andy is a pleasant guy, non-judgmental and very friendly. We would actually would call him very easy going and slow to anger. You have to do a lot to make Andy mad, a whole lot.

Andy can only testify to his experience, he does not hold all the answers. Many people come back from near death experiences with a lot of questions; *Why me? What is my purpose? Why did I come back?* Andy's purpose seemed to be the battle with his soon-to-be ex-wife. She was trying to kill him, have him unplugged. But was this the real reason or does Andy have more purpose, yet to be revealed? There's no real answer for this since only the omnipresent God knows the entire story. He sees the past, present and future. Trusting in his wisdom and goodness is the only answer. Faith in the unseen, yet to be revealed may be the answer.

Although this is a true story, because it's so personal, names and places have been changed in the book to protect people's identities. Andy thought it would give him more freedom to tell the entire story from his point of view. Co-authors Shane Flynn and Madeline Duffy tell the story of Andrew Fannon.

.

BACK TO THE BEGINNING

Click, click, click. A solid, loud sound is coming from my shoes. I'm walking down a large white hallway, possibly made of marble or some other hard substance that's making my shoes echo with a loud clicking sound, similar to metal hitting stone. It echoes in my head, sounding louder than it is, because I soon realize there's absolute silence. No other sound - other than the clicking of my heels, *click, click, click*. It's methodical and steady. Not really fast paced, but not slow either - just the strong, steady sound of *click, click, click*.

Even though this event happened about six years ago, it never completely leaves my mind. I've actually passed the 6 year anniversary of my near death experience and am in the 7th year. It hits me rather strange that I'm recording this event in its 7th year. Seven is an important number in the Bible. Seven represents completion and a day of rest. Interesting bit

of trivia there, isn't it? Numbers in the Bible have always fascinated me. I didn't really plan to put this into writing in the 7th year, it just sort of happened that way.

The memory of my two near death experiences are always there, stowed away in the background somewhere. They pop out on a regular basis, sometimes when I come across something that reminds me of them or sometimes when I'm supposed to tell another person about it. Maybe an angel taps me on the shoulder and whispers in my ear – not sure. But, regardless, it's always lurking somewhere, just waiting to be revealed.

People are always fascinated by my story. They listen intently and sometimes say "Wow". Some people will ask me questions about it and others are just fascinated by it. I don't find it leading into a big discussion about God usually, but the story seems to stand on its own. Maybe a seed being planted, I'm not sure. But people do like to hear about it and always listen intently. I can't remember anyone ever cutting me off or getting up to walk away. I tell it to anyone who cares enough to listen. I also don't remember anyone discrediting me or saying that they didn't believe it really happened. I feel called to tell it for some reason. I usually only tell people about the second experience. It seems to be the one that's supposed to be the most important and needs to be told.

THE WHITE SUIT

I'm including both experiences here, so you are the judge.

I hope the story conveys itself in writing as well as it does in person. Most people I've told know me in some way. Since you don't know me and can't see me, I'll have to tell you some things about myself. I'm now 64 years old and am very healthy. Some of the impact of the experience might be from people seeing me as I am today, healthy and happy. – I guess I'll just have to tell you that from the beginning. When I'm sitting telling someone the story, just looking at me says something, somehow. I'm fine and doing well. I have no lingering side effects and take no regular medication of any kind. I hesitate to even take an aspirin. Oh my stomach acts up once in a while, so I do take something for that, mostly because I don't eat as well as I should. I do love a good steak cooked on the grill! *Hah!*

Although I do have a good sense of humor, when you hear me say "Hah", it's more of an expression of surprise or exhilaration rather than meaning something's funny. I guess sometimes it could be interpreted as meaning something's funny, but more often it's something that's odd or surprising. It's not meant in a disrespectful way but more of a "isn't that amazing" kind of way.

My near death experience is an event that's so important to me, it's changed my life and how I live day to day, up to the present. Things just took on

different proportions. I guess once you visit the afterlife in person, things in the world all seem small and carry less importance in comparison.

You know, a lot of people might stop right now and think *Oh...here we go...another one of those "go to the light" stories,* especially due to the commonality of these many stories. Yes, you will find my *light story* here - however it takes on a much different set of circumstances. First of all I'm not a pastor or related to a pastor. I believe the commonality of these experiences only give proof to all of these stories and I believe God is showing His people a preview to one of life's biggest events and fears – that of death and what happens. I also think He wants us to share these experiences and spread the word to all who will listen.

Do you think God has chosen a variety of people to give these experiences to? I suppose I'm living proof that he has. I've also heard about some people that have dark messages or even visits to hell. My opinion is that if it brings you closer to God, it's real; all others are from the dark side. There is a battle going on here, on planet earth. Good vs. evil. I believe we all should review these experiences compared to the love of God. If God and his love are there, it's probably ok. Here's my story – you decide.

Do you believe in God? Do you believe he sent his son Jesus to die for our sins, so that we may stand clean and blameless before Him? Well, as far back as I can

THE WHITE SUIT

remember, I've always believed that. My family attended church, First Baptist and then Presbyterian. I went to a Baptist boarding school and I was required to attend the church of my choosing, which for me was a short walk to the local Presbyterian Church in San Antonio, Texas. Believing in Jesus Christ was a way of life for me. I don't remember any big *born again* moment as some people do. It was just simply a part of my life growing up. Like eating and drinking, just part of my everyday life. Since then I've found myself drifting away from the physical church for various reasons that I'll discuss as we go along. But my core belief in God and Christ has never wavered either before or after the experiences. As a matter of fact my belief felt confirmed and got stronger after the experience.

Some things are so solid in your life, that you do them without consciously thinking much about them. If you asked me about my conversation with God yesterday, I'm not sure I could tell you what we talked about. I know we talked, but I probably couldn't tell you about what exactly. We talk often, pretty much daily.

God just sort of hangs around my life somehow. He's always there and always listening. I think he talks back to me, just not in the same way you would talk to another person, it's different somehow. Something I hear inside of me. I really don't know what I'd do

without God to talk to. He doesn't judge me or criticize me - He listens and tries to help. When I say tries to help, I mean that He's the all-powerful God of the Universe, and he could force anything He wants on anyone. After all, if he's powerful enough to create things, that's real true power.

But my God isn't like that. He's more like the best father I could ever have - more like my friend and good buddy. He loves me unconditionally and completely. As I think back in time, He's always been there for me in some way or another. When I'm in trouble, he seems to help me out of it somehow. Best friend I ever had or will have.

I believe that once you accept Jesus Christ into your heart, your sins are forgiven. And I'm talking about past, present and future. God knows what we're going to do before we even think about doing it. I've always tried to live a decent life and I'm a nice, friendly guy. I don't try and break the law and I always want things to go along smoothly. But quite often things don't go along smoothly in life and you find yourself in situations that you never thought you'd be in. Some of them from bad choices, some are caused by others, and some are just random acts from the dark side.

God doesn't want a bunch of robots. He wants a personal relationship with his children. We aren't always perfect and He knows that. But He does love us and I'm so glad that He does.

THE WHITE SUIT

What defines your life? Are they the good things, the bad things, or a combination of both? I've found that some of the rough times and the bad things that happen seem to have more of an impact on your life. They challenge you, hurt you and by default, take you to new levels of understanding. So, you might find me citing more bad things because they impacted me more. But do understand that I'm a happy guy and have led a good life.

Do I think God causes or predestines these things? No, I don't. I believe God does have the ultimate power to allow or disallow these things because, He's all powerful. But as a child of God, I think God wants us to grow up and be good human beings. His greatest wish for us is to graduate to a higher level of understanding. My opinion is that life takes us on that journey - a journey toward understanding.

Ultimately, we get to choose whether to accept His presence or reject it. That's God's gift to us. We have the freedom of choice. But I also believe He is a good God and gives us more than ample opportunity to make the right choice. That He has created a "hole" in us that only He can fill. We can search the world looking for something to fill it, but material things come up short and don't fill the hole for very long. Do we all learn at different speeds and through different experiences? I would have to say we do. Maybe I'm a slow learner or

maybe you can relate to my story. I guess we all have different paths to walk and I hope mine helps you.

You see, I was bullied as a child and sent off to boarding school at age fifteen. It's tough being bullied as a child, sort of affects your mind somehow. I guess we're all bullied at some time in our lives. It's not a pleasant experience, but makes you stronger I guess. At least Johnny Cash thought so when he wrote *A Boy Named Sue. Hah!*

No matter how many people try to say it's normal and common, I hate it. Young children shouldn't be made fun of, no matter what the circumstance. Bullying is perhaps your first sign as a child that the world's a cruel place - a place to be feared - that other people can pose a danger to you - and should be checked out carefully before entrusting them. People and words can be dangerous. Words are powerful and they can be used for good or bad; and they can be used to hurt people deep inside. The power of the tongue! *Hah!*

Now, don't go thinking of me as a victim, my life *is what it is*. I certainly don't think of myself as a victim. I've led a very good life, having its ups and downs like any other life on this planet. Everything that's part of my past helped me toward my future. (That's the history buff coming out in me). I'm pretty much just an ordinary guy that some people might call a "sinner".

THE WHITE SUIT

"Do I read the Bible?" you ask.

"Yes, sometimes."

I read it mandatorily in military school, I was invited to join a men's bible study in my 20's during my first marriage, and I know intellectually most of what it says. I've read it in its entirety a number of times, but more out of obligation than pleasure. Do I understand the deep meanings of the Bible? Does anyone ever understand all that is contained in that single book? I'll just leave it there.

I guess I believe that things from God's book are consistently being revealed as He sees fit. All part of life's journey I guess. It's a magical book – it's supernatural in power. You can read one passage one day and as life changes, read the same passage another day and discover a whole new meaning. It reminds me of a multi-faceted diamond -glowing and sparkling in many different directions all at once - beautiful and everlasting. But my one solid belief is that God is good. He's not this mean judgmental, high and mighty being just waiting to punish us. He's good and loving and wants to help us. Yep, that's the God I believe in. A good God.

But was I prepared to meet God, face to face? Not something I'd ever thought about I guess. I was busy going through life. Dealing with all the day to day issues; wives, making a living, eating, sleeping, and all the things we do every day. We never stop to think

about the fact that all those things might come to a grinding halt at some strange, inconvenient moment in time.

Click, click, click. There's that sound again, coming from my shoes hitting something solid, white and gleaming with a color that is a staggering bright white. From what I understand, black is the absence of light, and white is the combination of all colors. These colors can be broken apart through a prism and seen as a rainbow. *Where am I? What am I doing here?* That question is pressing on my mind. But it's peaceful with warm love. There's no fear, no dread. Nothing seems wrong; it seems more puzzling than anything else. *Click, click, click.* It feels like I'm walking down that white hallway for a very long time.

I told you, it's always there in the background of my mind.

"Where exactly does God fit into my story?" you might well ask.

I guess I should start at the beginning, or at least the beginning of this story, so that you can understand more clearly. More clearly about where my head is, more clearly about where my life is. How I got to this place and how events that're happening to me at this very moment will change me forever.

Why should we start at the beginning you ask? Well, things don't happen in a vacuum, they happen for a reason. Events in our lives are all intertwined; with a

THE WHITE SUIT

beginning, middle and end. If I only told you about my near death experience, I don't think you would understand it as a stand-alone event. It's part of my life and my death. I believe that near death experiences are personally made for each individual and in order to understand the experience, you have to take a look at the individual. Our God is like that, talks to us personally. If you have a near death experience, it will be entirely different, because you are different. It would be your own personal experience with the Almighty God.

So sit back, get to know me and maybe you'll understand my near death experiences. If you don't have an interest in me, skip ahead to the chapter that describes it. But you won't get full insight, if you make that choice. Interesting that I just gave you a choice - that's what I was given during my near death experience; a choice. I guess we all have choices that we make every day. Some of them are good choices that make our life easier and some are bad choices that make life harder. I suppose some of them are shaped by our past and how we search for love and acceptance. I wish I could say that all of my choices have been good, but that's not the case.

I guess this is a story about life and death. It's my story and I hope you won't be too hard on me. I've made lots of mistakes, but I'm just doing the best I can.

This is the life I've been given and the journey has been quite interesting.

I was a rather sickly child early on and my mom was very overprotective. Doctors thought I had Rheumatic Fever. I'm not sure if I did or not, as medicine was still rather basic in the 1950's. Mom was always taking me to the doctor and I was strictly prohibited from any strenuous activities. Also, there was always that lingering threat hanging around - that horrible disease - *polio*.

One of my parent's dear friend's sons contracted it at age eighteen. He was a senior in high schools and quarterback of the football team. He went from total health to living in an iron lung at night, paralyzed from the neck down. His name was Billy, and later in my teens, he became a good friend of mine. Billy was a truly remarkable young man, an artist actually. He would paint with his teeth and mouth, holding the brush and moving his head all around to brush the canvas.

Billy loved all us kids that would come by after school and help him with his art. There was an attachment to his gurney type of *chair* which would allow a canvas to hang over his face. He would tell us which color of paint to put on the palette and then take the brush in his mouth, dab the color and then apply it to the canvas. His paintings were incredible and so highly detailed that one wouldn't believe a quadriplegic painted them - detailed down to a single blade of grass.

THE WHITE SUIT

He gave a lot of paintings away and sold some, with the sales helping to finance his care.

He was truly a man of God and such an inspiration to whomever knew him. Billy introduced me to model airplanes and model making in general, which became a lifetime hobby for me. A friend of the family built him a gym, right across the street from his house. Billy invited all the football players to come lift weights at his gym. There was always a lot of activity at Billy's gym. It was an incredible, inspirational place. The strong and the weak united in total kindness and compassion.

Billy went to be with the Lord only about five years ago, just shortly after his parents and after forty years in that 'chair' and sleeping in an iron lung at night. People come and go out of our lives, some leaving lasting impressions. Billy was one of those *lasting impressions*, someone I hope to see again and take a walk with, down golden streets. It'll be nice to see him out of that *chair*, walking and laughing with a new body fully intact. Just thinking about him makes me tear up. Billy touched my heart in many ways.

As for me, I was never able to do many things that kids my age were doing, such as organized football, baseball, swimming or similar sports. This's where the bullying comes into play - I was different from the rest of the other kids. I could play *gently* around the

neighborhood, but nothing organized at school or in the community. I might get hurt.

My mom, she hated the sun. She wore long sleeve blouses with high necks. I don't know why she disliked sunshine, maybe for her skin, I really don't know. She was a rather vain woman and old fashioned. I don't mean that in a bad way, she was a lovely woman, and I guess she liked that part about herself. We lived in south Texas and the sun is really hot most of the time - cloudy days are rare. Even in her later years, she always carried a newspaper with her to shield her from the sun when she ran into the store to pick up something.

This is one thing that I'm glad I didn't inherit. I love the sun and a good tan. I sunbath frequently when I can. Being of Irish decent means that my skin is inherently pale. A good tan really makes me feel rather *dapper. Hah!*

Although some of the things I talk about in my life seem bad, I don't consider them bad at all. I think I've had a good and interesting journey. It's not perfect but it's not been boring either.

I had two parents that I felt loved me, an inconvenience to them at times, but loved none the less. They didn't beat me or starve me. They were basic moral, ethical parents. My mother loved me as best she could. I don't think she knew the full meaning of love, but they both did the best they knew how to do. When

THE WHITE SUIT

my mom sent me off to military school, it hurt me a lot. It felt as if she was trying to get rid of me, that I was an inconvenience. I felt deserted and unloved as I made that trip to the new school.

Back in the 1950's it was quite popular to send your kids away to boarding school. I think things have changed since then. People are keeping their kids close to home. I'm not sure if the social status surrounding it changed or people just couldn't afford to do it anymore. Regardless, kids stay home now, which I consider a change for the better. Kids belong at home.

These feelings of abandonment would subside as I adjusted to new friends and a new life in a school without parents. I now had officers that took over the role as parents. Sure, a lot of things were different, but I tried to adjust. There were a lot of rules and procedures. If you didn't follow the rules, there was discipline. Food was dished out cafeteria style, and it wasn't very good. I remember my favorite being hamburgers. After all, it's not easy to totally destroy a hamburger. My least favorite was the chipped beef on toast, *shit on a shingle* is what most military called it. I still don't eat it to this day. I've found this to be typical military taste; they leave creamed chipped beef behind in the military where they first found it. *Hah! Good riddance to creamed chipped beef!*

I spent three years at that school. I made some good friends, but I missed the feeling of the family and

I missed some of my friends from back home. It was an experience that I would never put a child of my own through; however, it's an experience that I would never trade either. It was probably there that I gained an independence that I might never have otherwise and that would prove to be invaluable later in life.

It was about a three hour drive from my small home town in south Texas to my new military school. My parents would drive up and visit from time to time. They were members of a private club located in one of the old hotels down on the river in San Antonio. They'd feature many of the old ballroom Big Bands from the 40's such as Vince Lombardo and at least once a month. When they were there, we went out to dinner at the club, and they usually went dancing after dinner. They both loved to dance. I wouldn't stay and watch them dance, but rather hook up with my new friends or just be by myself and go out exploring the town. I guess in hindsight, my relationship with my parents was rather detached. We all loved each other, but in a somewhat distant, formal kind of way.

Perhaps my parent's definition of love was only defined by what they knew from their parents or perhaps they tried even harder than they had known. I'm not sure about that, not having lived their lives. We all seem to live imperfect lives, especially when it comes to love. I guess the only perfect love is the real

THE WHITE SUIT

and only true definition of love, and that is God himself.

There's no *Beaver Cleaver or Ozzie and Harriett* kind of family. Well, if there is, they aren't on every street corner. And I didn't have one of those *perfect, loving families*.

My parents didn't have siblings that they interacted with. My mother had fallen out with her family. I never knew the exact reason why, but it was a permanent falling out. Her sister started out dating my dad after the war (WWII) and when they broke up, my mom stepped in. I think that might have had something to do with the *falling out*. They didn't speak or show up on holidays. In fact, Mom was so estranged from her family that my grandmother, whom I hadn't seen since I was about 7-8 years old, had died, and it was over three years later when she told me about it. When one of her sisters died, I read about it in the paper well after her funeral and after another sister died, she was so mad at me for telling her about it, that she wouldn't speak to me for 3 weeks. I actually think that inside she was ashamed of her family, among other reasons which I'll never know. My dad's family was very limited too. He seemed to always think that it was up to him to take care of them, at least his five sisters, anyway. Dad only had one brother and he was very close to him, and I do have a relationship with their son, my cousin. Oddly enough, neither of us had

children, so the family name will die with us. My extended family was extremely small. We didn't have big family gatherings except at funerals and the last one I went to – or even knew about was my grandmother's (dad's mom) back in 1967. It was mainly just me and my parents. I was an only child. I was spoiled in some ways, neglected in others.

Now my dad was a Cadillac kind of guy. He loved Cadillac's - paid cash for every single one he owned. Dad paid cash for everything. He didn't believe in credit. He bought his first Cadillac in 1961, a white Coupe de Ville with a pink interior - Mom's favorite color. Let me tell you about my dad and his love for cars. I bet he owned twenty Cadillac's in his lifetime. As a matter of fact, after his death, my mom was published in a book about Cadillac owners published by General Motors. He owned some of the most bizarre vehicles. I remember one that had been special ordered by a friend of his back in 1984, the guy decided he didn't like it and returned it - and good ole Dad found it on the car lot. It was bright yellow on the outside and royal blue on the inside and had a blue vinyl top. A giant Fleetwood Brougham with chrome wire wheels. It even had a built in CB radio which was really popular back then. You talk about an eye-catcher, it was downright gaudy. You couldn't miss him cruising down the street in his yellow and blue Caddie! I think

THE WHITE SUIT

he owned every color in the rainbow by the time he left this world.

My mom, she loved pink. She painted the outside of the house hot pink, including the flower boxes. We had pink bathrooms, pink dishes and pink everywhere. The funny thing about my parents was that they respected each other's taste in color. Neither criticized the other for their wild color palettes. I guess I lived a colorful life in some respects. Overall my parents were kind, generous people. I guess that's my favorite memory of them - yep, kind and generous people.

Dad, he saved his money. He worked hard in the oil business and they were upper middle class. That was a time when the individual small businessman could make a really good living doing his own thing. My dad would say "Andy, always be in business for yourself. If your head is in the ground and your butt is in the air - that means you're workin' for *THE MAN.*"

I'm an only child. Only children don't have brothers and sisters to play with or fight with - we live in a world of adults. As a child I built my first model ship, the *Charles W. Morgan*, a whaling ship. It was a plastic model that kept me occupied as an only child. I would spend hours and hours working on all the perfect details - made me love the water and making things and ships of the era. I've heard it called "back in the time of wooden ships and iron men".

SHANE FLYNN & MADELINE DUFFY

Yeah, I had some neighborhood friends that I played with. Ned and Bud were my best friends who lived down the street. We're still friends to this day. We played baseball together in a small park in a small town. Bud and I once fought over a baseball - we were about 9 or 10 years old. Both of us felt that we had brought the baseball to the field that day. We fought over it and I ended up winning the battle. Glowing, home I went - baseball in hand.

For years Bud and I laughed over that story, how we fought over that baseball as young tikes. Many years later, I would find that very baseball in my Mother's attic, even the box was there. Bud and I had grown into mature businessmen by then, and I stopped by Bud's office, presenting him with the disputed baseball. I told him it was his turn to take care of it now, I had it long enough. We had a good laugh about the good ole days. *Hah!*

Ned moved away for a few years but returned in his early teens. Ned and Bud became brothers to me - only children seem to do that sort of thing. Since they don't have their own siblings, they tend to adopt some. I still feel today that Ned and Bud are my brothers. We've kept up with each other through the years and sometimes through many marriages. Do we see each other every day or even every year? No we don't see each other for many years sometimes, but still the feeling remains. We're brothers that grew up together

THE WHITE SUIT

and when we do see each other, it's very comfortable, like family. I don't think that will ever change.

For many years my parents lived in a small two bedroom house, simple but nice. When Dad saved up enough money, he went out and had a custom designed house built for he and Mom. Can you imagine paying cash for a house today? It was a really nice house too, four bedrooms and roomy. I was home from the Navy by then and helped build that house. I learned a lot from the builder - how to make cabinets, how to frame a building - so much that it would turn out to be a fundamental part of who I was becoming as a man. I can build almost anything now. Just give me the right tools and materials - I can build it.

The contractor was a German craftsman to the nth degree. He, his brother, a cousin and two laborers would build houses in south Texas. They'd only build one at a time from start to finish and then move on to the next. They were the only quality builders in the area, therefore had a waiting list that went out 4-5 years….you just get in line and they'd eventually get to you. Well, it was my parent's time, and they really built a nice house.

Dad always wanted me to go to college. I tried at first, but just couldn't get serious about it for some reason. That's when I joined the Navy. I was off to see the world. My parents were not happy with my decision. It was probably their biggest disappointment

in me. As an only child, all expectations fell solely on me, no siblings to take the pressure off. But they eventually fell in line and even came aboard my air craft carrier for a big event once. I think they were secretly proud of me. I was getting more discipline and actually growing up into the mature man I would become.

I suppose I should explain how I got to the Navy in the first place. This goes back to my first attempt at college after my very strict stint at a confined boarding school. You know - the military school. Well, after military school, I came back home and I enrolled at a local college in south Texas.

Later I realized that my dad had spent a lot of money in an attempt to educate me. Dad only had an eighth grade education, yet was quite successful in his endeavors. He all but demanded that I get a college degree and I took advantage of his generosity and squandered, partied and played my way into flunking out.

Dad was hard to hold a conversation with. He mostly lectured. It was annoying sometimes. Maybe I became a good listener from him. I sat and listened, he lectured.

Now bear in mind that this is the Viet Nam War era. Not in school? - off to Nam. This is not a good place to go, but too late. Ned and I were roommates at this time, going to college, both flunking out at the

THE WHITE SUIT

same time. We'd been childhood friends and were both former military school kids, him going to a different school in the Texas Hill Country. It was party time back then and we paid the price!

Ned's uncle was a Colonel in the Air Force National Guard in Arkansas. We called Uncle Brad to see if he could get us into the Air Force. He told us to come to Arkansas and he'd see what he could do - so we went to Arkansas. We just left college, we didn't drop out, we just left. This would be something that I would regret later on in life. Well, we turned out to be about six months too old. He called another friend in the Navy - next thing we knew – we were sailors. We went back to our house in Texas to move and tell our parents what we did. I think Dad was pretty disgusted by this point and he didn't care one way or the other. He just said, "I hope you know what you're doing"……that was it.

Ned and I went to Navy school together and then he shipped out. I stayed at school a while longer and then I shipped out on an air craft carrier. As I climb aboard, I take a deep breath of salt water infused air mixed with a sour fish smell. Yum, this was my new life for the next two years. As I'm looking around this massive gray painted behemoth of a ship, the newest and greatest carrier of the fleet, I'm surprised when I catch a glimpse of DJ.

SHANE FLYNN & MADELINE DUFFY

You see, DJ and I'd met previously in boot camp, but discovered each other again aboard the carrier. We became fast friends after that. The Navy was a big influence on me - the military is something that becomes part of you. It never leaves you, even after you leave it. I can't say that I wanted to stay for a lifetime and I was glad to get out. Actually DJ and I got out (or escaped) at the same time. How is that for coincidence? That was actually quite an experience on its own. We were in the Mediterranean on deployment. Actually during this time the powers that be were escalating the war in Viet Nam. They began sending all of the bombs, fuel and other assets to support the escalation. What that meant for us was that we would pull into certain ports and be anchored for up to six weeks at a time. So essentially, I spent six weeks in Barcelona, six weeks in Palma de Mallorca, six weeks in Athens, and six weeks on the Isle of Rhodes.

My Navy friend DJ and I camped in places that almost killed us. You'll like this one. We were camping in a pup tent one night along the beach at Ocracoke Island in North Carolina. It was my twenty second birthday. There was a celebration of barbequed hot dogs and beer around the campfire. After a night of laughter, food and drink we crawled into our sleeping bags and fell fast asleep. Suddenly, we found ourselves waking up to someone or something beating on us with sticks. *Thump...whack...thump...whack!* It took a few

THE WHITE SUIT

minutes for us to realize that the reason we were being beat, was that our pup tent had collapsed and the two end poles were flapping in the wind and beating on us. *Hah!*

Apparently a tropical storm had come ashore, Tropical Storm Arlene to be exact. Arlene had hung offshore for a few days and eventually developed into a tropical storm. Our tent was in shambles all around us. We scrambled to put it back together, but with no luck. It was storming and pouring down rain. DJ and I were soaked - we slept in the car that night - all curled up in a Cadet Opal. Needless to say, if you know what an Opal looks like - it was small, tight, and uncomfortable quarters. *Hah!*

Yep, those were adventurous times for DJ and me. We didn't have much money, considering a Navy pay of about $150 a month. But we made the most of it, touring Spain, Italy, Greece, France, Turkey and a few others. Seeing the Pope at the Vatican on Christmas Day was an extraordinary high point in our travels. DJ and I were standing along one side of St. Peter's Square - isn't it interesting that it's called a Square when it's actually a circle? Suddenly we hear the sound of someone opening the windows above us and a large purple tapestry gloriously rolled down. We then realize that we have unknowingly picked the perfect spot to see the Pope. About twenty minutes later, Pope Paul VI appears and gives his Christmas blessing to the

crowd. There may have been twenty to thirty thousand people there. These days there are more like one hundred thousand people attending this event. How lucky could we get? Here we are, two Navy seamen being blessed by the Pope on Christmas Day. All is in Italian of course, and we can't understand a word being said, but it's one of the most moving experiences of my lifetime. There was a presence there; I guess the presence of God.

DJ and I laughed together over many a glass of beer in many different countries and in many different situations. Even today, when I get together with DJ, it seems like no time has really passed. We pick up right where we left off, good friends who enjoy each other's company.

We both decided to apply for an *early out* in order to go to college in Indiana. We got approved for a two month early release from active duty so that we could do so. The problem is that the ship was supposed to return to Norfolk in June and we would have plenty of time to be separated from the service and get back to Indiana in time to start class. Well, since the escalation was in process, the ship's deployment was extended and we weren't going to return on time. So the Navy, in its omnipotence, decides that since there are about 10 of us on board to be separated from the Navy, they will pull into Izmir, Turkey to let us out. We pull into Izmir, they anchor offshore, put 10 of us into a Liberty

THE WHITE SUIT

Boat (basically a launch for taking sailors to and from the dock when in a port), with all our belongings, take us ashore, and leave. Here we are in Izmir, Turkey and there's absolutely no one that speaks English, yet alone wondering what the heck we're doing there. This is also the first time a US ship has come into the port in Izmir in about 15 years. It seems the last time the Navy was there, an incident occurred where the Turks (mostly Turkish Army) literally threw the American sailors into the water off of the dock and under protest, the US pulled out of Turkey, never to return until we showed up. The US has an airbase up in the mountains of Turkey run by the Air Force and we're supposed to contact the Air Force to transport us by MAC (Military Airlift Command) back to the US to get separated from the service so we can enroll in school.

So, we've just been dumped out in Turkey. No one but Turkish Army guys around us, no one speaks English, we're about 20 miles from downtown Izmir, we're on foot, and I have two sea bags, two guitars, and two Beretta Over and Under 12 gauge shotguns, boxed, that I got in Italy at the factory, that I'm trying to carry somewhere, but have no idea where. A decision to buy souvenirs and gifts turned terribly wrong when we get dumped instead of transported by ship as originally planned.

We're being "eyed" by the locals and I now understand the power of being in a group and also the

power of being US military…..ten disoriented sailors, but a group at least. There's no one here to greet or help us that look friendly, much less Air Force. We're totally unarmed and I don't even have any shells for the two shotguns in the boxes. Now what?

Interesting enough, a few years ago, while in engineering school at college, I had a teacher who was a Turk. And he loved to talk. He'd warned me about the brutality of the Turkish Army. Luckily this gave me some background on the place and I knew not to get into any skirmishes with their Army. I kind of wonder if God sent that teacher ahead to warn me, because he knew I'd be in Turkey someday. Hadn't thought about that till now -sure is interesting.

We group up realizing that we're basically in hostile territory. No one likes us here. We look back at the Carrier and realize it's pulling out of Izmir and we're on our own. Someone talks to some Turk that understands a couple of words of English who thinks there's an Air Force office about a mile down the road. So off we go trying to get to this AF office to find out what we're supposed to do. Such fun, I feel like a donkey with all this stuff, one sea bag on each shoulder, each about 40 lbs., two guitars in each hand in cases, and a shotgun under each armpit…..and I've gotta walk a mile yet. On top of that we're all very uncomfortable with our surroundings. We revert back to the military training and look at each other to determine rank.

THE WHITE SUIT

We're all a bunch of enlisted guys with our highest rank being a 2nd class Petty Officer (E5). Like a "Who's in charge situation." Well, we're in trouble….we're like a covey of quail bunching up….no leader. We do manage to get to the Air Force office in a couple of hours and find at least someone who speaks English. He's an E3 guard and has absolutely no idea or paperwork as to why we're there. The Air Force evidently didn't get the paper work to process us, much less fly us back to the States. He tries to call (landline) the base in the mountains to ask his boss what to do with us. The phone lines are primitive to say the least, and of course, don't work. So once again here we are in hostile territory. He tells us to find a hotel, camp out, sleep outside the office on the ground or just go away….he didn't care. He would try to find out what to do with us, but no promises. He said the next bus from Izmir to the AF base would be 3 days from now.

Fortunately, DJ and I had saved two of our paychecks for spending money. We look at each other, and decide we should find a taxi if possible. We eventually flag down a very reluctant taxi driver. DJ and I have separated from the group like most everyone. We all decide we are on our own. Since I have the most junk with me DJ and I got abandoned…..all men for themselves. Our taxi driver knew just a little bit of English…such as *hotel*. I think that might've been his limits, but it worked. He took us

to the Izmir Hilton in downtown Izmir, probably the best hotel in Izmir. We have no idea what we paid since all we have are US dollars and not Turkish Lira. They say the Lira will actually float on water, so to say the least it was pretty worthless, and dollars talked.

We checked into the hotel, and all we want is a good cold beer. Once we are in our room we head to the bar. If you think the French are rude you should have seen the service...or lack of it that we got at the hotel bar. We're totally ignored for well over thirty minutes until someone in our group of about six (since most of us ended up at the same place) actually grabbed one of the waiters by the collar, pulled him up almost face to face and yelled at him that we wanted a beer. He reluctantly stumbled off to the bar mumbling all kinds of gibberish in Turkish as he went. He brought back five or six beers of some sort...we worried about what was in it, but we got a beer. Getting the second one was a repeat of the first experience - lovely place. If you've never felt unwanted in a primitive foreign county, it's an experience for sure. You have to keep the fear bottled up and put on a strong outward appearance.

Once figuring out that the Air Force had no clue what to do with us, DJ and I, having saved two paychecks, decide we're going to book a flight to New York, rent a car and drive to Norfolk. This is where DJ's little Opal car is, and we know how to get there -

THE WHITE SUIT

we can get processed out of the Navy fast enough to make it for school in Indiana. So that's our plan. Next morning we get up, manage to get a taxi to the airport, get to the terminal TWA flight to Athens, change planes and straight to New York, La Guardia with a refuel stop in Shannon, Ireland. I hate Turkey and never wanted to see it again. Later I would return.

Alright, so we accomplish this part of getting back to the states. We get to Athens, get our baggage, and transfer it to the US terminal of TWA. They don't automatically transfer your baggage and we have to take it ourselves about a half mile to the next terminal. Now imagine this in today's world. We're at the Athens, Greece airport; I'm carrying my two sea bags, two guitars and two shotguns through the airport on an international flight....hmmm. Try that now. *Hah!*

The one upside is we have to fly in full dress blue uniforms. So here we are, two very tired sailors boarding a long flight back to the US. Viet Nam is not a popular war and military personnel in this period are pretty much shunned by everyone....scum. Well this little stewardess, flight attendant in today's terminology, felt sorry for us and pulled us aside and said she had two first class seats that she was going to put us in. Wow, we got free drinks and good food for the first time in...I don't know how long. She took care of us and we both were in love. We stopped in Shannon, and I bought my mother a bottle of old Irish whiskey in a clay crock. Tullimore's Dew, I think was the name of it. My mother loved Irish coffee. That's another story too of course.

Upon arrival in New York, we rent a car and head to Norfolk. It takes about a week to process us out and off we go to Indianapolis.

We go to DJ's home town in Indiana and we're getting ready to return to college. Well things didn't work out so well in Indiana because we wound up being 10 days too late to enroll, and after a bit I ended up back in south Texas. I left that bottle of Irish whiskey in Indiana and interesting enough it found its way back to Texas over 20 odd years later when DJ visited.

I am living at my parent's house for a while - I can go back to college here, having already been enrolled there before the Navy. I now have a problem though. Remember when we quit school to join the Navy a few years back? - I had an entire 15 hours of F's on my transcript. They were all Electrical Engineering classes. I am allowed in, but on Scholastic Probation. I can retake the classes and get a passing grade to get them removed or replaced, but they have to remain on my records. At this point I have no interest at all in EE, I am there to get a degree in business. I now regret the way I exited college to go into the world. I'm going to pay for my recklessness. All I would've had to do was drop out and formally drop the classes to have not had

THE WHITE SUIT

any of this on my transcript. By doing what I did and just leaving, they all ended the semester as F's and I had to carry those throughout the rest of school. What an idiot I was. As it turns out, when I graduate with my BBA, I have exactly a 2.0 grade point which is the minimum you can graduate with because of this error in judgment. As you can see, I've made a lot of bad decisions and have made my life much harder than it needed to be.

I was determined to get that college degree but I was going to pay for it now. I wasn't going to take advantage of Dad anymore – I have earned the GI Bill, which can help pay for school. I use one hundred percent of my GI Bill and not only earned a Bachelors' Degree, but several Associates Degrees and eventually a Master's Degree. Since I work for myself during all of this, Dad can't understand why I went for the Masters, but he did understand the Bachelors. Maybe he was happy…not sure, not much recognition there, just acceptance. Doesn't matter, darn it…..I did it.

A friend of mine says that we all paddle in our own river of caca. I find this quite funny, but is it true? Are all our lives just a river of caca? Do we find ourselves frantically paddling to avoid being flushed out the rear end of life? *Hah!*

When I enroll in college, well that's where I meet Kate (my first wife) and we get married a little over a year later. I thought my parents loved Kate. I am married to her for eighteen long years. When things started going bad with Kate, I stay for a long time - I don't want to disappoint my parents. The fact that I met her on the day her divorce was final should've been my first clue.

You see when I meet Kate it's a blind date that my barber sets me up on. Actually, he set me up with one of her students named Cathy. On the night we are supposed to go out, Cathy calls me and says that she has a friend, whose divorce is final today that she would like to take her with us and that she will set her up with her old boyfriend for the night. I don't really care so that's what we do. Well, about half way through the date, Cathy decides she's really not over her old boyfriend yet. Then Kate and I start talking since our dates are ignoring us. Very soon we all change seats, and my date winds up with her old boyfriend and Kate and I are thrown together. We strike up a conversation, and very quickly into it we realize that while she was in college, I was in school with the Navy. Her hometown is where us sailors would go on weekends during liberty, or time off. Since we frequented the same bars in downtown at the exact same time, we probably even ran into each other back then, but had no idea.

She had married a guy in Navy ROTC at the university she graduated from. They got married and he received his commission as an Ensign in the US

THE WHITE SUIT

Navy. They were immediately transferred to Pensacola, Florida for OCS and flight school. He was a Navy pilot. She was the only family member that ever left the Midwest.

Paul, her husband was at the mercy of the Navy which determined his schedule, not Kate. This very quickly became a problem. She'd be working and he'd be out flying all over the country, sometimes for days at a time and this did not go over well. After about six or seven months it festered into a giant blow up. That year a major hurricane was headed toward Pensacola. The Navy flies their planes out of danger before any severe weather strikes a base. This sent Paul flying his plane to San Diego, California until the storm passed, which was five to ten days. This didn't go over well with the newlywed bride. They owned a trailer house, had a dog and a 1956 Chevy which was not in good shape. Kate now had to withstand a hurricane for the first time in her life….by herself while her husband flew off to safety and spends the next week hanging out in the Officer's Club, drinking and cavorting. Not a good scenario.

Bottom line here is that she was married to him, and he was married to the Navy. She packed up the Irish Setter, the 56 Chevy and drove as far west and south as she could. She ended up in south Texas, found a junior college, applied for a job and was accepted. Kate went back to Florida, packed up her stuff, moved to south Texas and filed for divorce. We met the day the divorce was final, six months later.

Kate was a college professor when I met her and I was a college senior. We married a year and a half later. I got a job offer in Houston and off we went.

After moving to Houston, I work for a company for a while and after that I always worked for myself, oil business mostly. We make a good living, have a few good friends and travel a lot, no children. Kate and I decide early on, not to have children. Both being only kids, we like the freedom of traveling and generally doing *our own thing*. Children sound like a burden, something you have to take care of.

I guess my mother instilled this feeling in me. I always felt somewhat of a burden to her. I was something that held her back from her social life. I just don't think she knew any better. She loved me in her own way. Perhaps this influenced me in my decision about not having children. Kate and I are enjoying our freedom. We are having fun. In fact I've been to Hawaii twenty three times, between my two marriages.

Kate has her own reasons for not wanting children. She'd come from an abusive home and also was an only child. She grew up as I had in that regard, spending a lot of time alone and entertaining myself. She was born and raised in a big Midwestern city. Her parents were blue collar and were both members of their respective unions. Her father worked for the city

THE WHITE SUIT

and her mother was a checker for the local supermarket chain. Being Polish they had their own discriminatory issues to deal with. They were very socialistic in their thinking and politics.

Kate's grandparents actually came to the US just prior to World War II and settled in the Midwest. They were good Polish Catholics and escaped the war and Polish occupation by the Nazi's. Kate's mother married young in the early part of the war, in a quick romance, to a Polish-American man and US Army GI being shipped out to Germany a week after they married. Within a month of his deployment she got the dreaded telegram stating that he had been killed in action. This was pretty traumatic to her. Needless to say and she didn't remarry until a few years after the war ended.

Kate's father also was a GI and served in Germany too. All I know about his experience is that he went through some very traumatic and intense hand to hand combat battles, many times, and survived. After the war it really affected his social skills and he became very meek, timid, reclusive and secretive, never telling his story. I only found out a little of it through Kate's only uncle and he knew very little. Personally I think it's bad to keep deep dark secrets, they should be brought out into the light for healing.

Ten years went by and our freedom turned into Kate's domination over me. This seemed to manifest after the oil market crashed due to new taxation put into effect by Jimmy Carter. I don't know if she got scared or what exactly affected her. My oil business dropped. Even though we had plenty of money, this market crash did something to her.

She used control and anger, with maybe some OCD mixed in. She got so bad that if a vase wasn't put back in exactly, and I mean exactly the same place after cleaning, she would have a fit - a big, loud fit. After all, Kate came from a blue collar, 9 to 5 family. Work was security, a paycheck. She followed that ideology and worked a regular 9 to 5 job. Her idea of a job meant that you left the house and went to an office of some kind. You see, *since I didn't work, not a real job any more (in her opinion);* I worked for myself selling oil field equipment and had a small landscaping company - then I was *put* in charge of the house and yard. For example, after working all day cleaning the house, Kate would come home after her classes and inspect. If the vase was not <u>exactly</u> in the right spot, it would infuriate her. She would insult and chew me up one side and down the other. She could make you feel you didn't even exist and you were the scum of the earth.

We had a large glass dining room table. It had four candles in the center under the chandelier. She took a string and attached it to the center crystal piece of the chandelier and found the <u>exact</u> center of the table.

THE WHITE SUIT

Then she took paper and drew each candle and where it was located on the table. This was where she wanted everything placed. When she inspected the table after I'd cleaned the glass for any dust and fingerprints, she would break out the string and blueprint to verify everything was perfectly placed. If not, *look out*, here it comes. It was the same for the yard. I wasn't *allowed* to hire help or yard maintenance people. After all, *I didn't work* remember, and she would say "Do you know how many hours I have to work to pay for that?"

Bear in mind, I made my money in chunks. If I sold a piece of equipment, I might make $5000 to $10,000. The profit on one item could be very high, which at the time could be more than she was making as a college professor. But, that didn't seem to count. Do you think this was just maybe OCD and a control problem? *Hah!* Hen-pecked doesn't even begin to describe how I felt - it went way beyond that cliché.

You know, I suppose some people could see this situation as a weakness on my part – and actually, I guess it was. An abusive situation, especially verbal and emotional abuse, is something that gradually happens and tends to brainwash you into a submissive nature. You eventually believe what they say to you and about you. By gradually, I mean over a couple of years and more – in my case over eighteen years. My final experience with her OCD over the vase, candles and chandelier was a *light bulb moment*. I never saw most of this occurring and only after I was out of the relationship was it revealed to me fully. Wow, I not only realized it, but also realized that I had wasted the last ten years of my life – my prime of life at that. Things changed way back when that ring went on the finger and it took me a long time to see it.

After 18 years when I finally couldn't take the marriage with Kate anymore and decided to give it up, I reluctantly called my parents. I mean, I was scared to call them, petrified even. I put it off for weeks. I was expecting them to be upset and disappointed in me. That was becoming a constant for me, disappointing my parents.

Surprisingly, my dad's first response was, "What the hell took you so –blank-blank long? Never did like her."

Hah! Life is never what you expect! Here he hated her. He was so happy that I finally saw the light. *Hah!* I guess you never know what's in other people's minds, not even your own parents.

Mom said "I loved her because she was your wife, but I never liked her."

Hah again! It was a relief to hear them say those words. Now my divorce from Kate could be done with my family's full support. What a surprise that was!

Unfortunately, dad went to sing in the choir that year and never saw the divorce get finalized. That's

THE WHITE SUIT

really where he told us he was going as he passed....to sing in the choir. He looked up toward the sky and said he was going to go sing. Although he wasn't the best singer, he always sang in our local church. It was something he loved.

My parents had been married for a long time. I couldn't imagine my parents not being married to one another. Even after my father's death, my mother grieved him. She became a recluse and just pined for my father. She lived seventeen years after my father's death and things never changed. My mom cut off all her old friends and just pined away to be with my dad. I tried to encourage her toward other things, but it always ended up the same. I gave up and accepted it after a few years. Mom was just going to be Mom, and that was that.

I bet Mom and Dad had a grand meeting in 2010, dancing their way around Heaven. Mom's burial clothes were her dancing clothes, so when she went to meet him, she was ready to dance. Remember that clay crock bottle of Tullimore's Dew Irish Whiskey? I bought it in 1972 and DJ brought it back to Mom in 1998 when he visited me. Mom never opened it, so the day of Mom's funeral, I cracked it open and we had a toast to Mom. Go dancing Mom....go Dancing!

Why have I told you all of this? Well, you can't appreciate a near death experience or hope to understand it, unless you know the person. I hope that

I've given you enough background information on me that you now feel that you know me, at least a little. It's hard to put your whole life's story into one chapter, but I've tried to hit the high and low points, depending on your how you look at it.

CAITE

Here I am, sitting in a darkened, smoke filled bar, slowly sipping a wonderfully aged Single Malt Scotch and relishing a prime Cuban cigar. It's a cool day in Houston and is too cold to sit outside. I'm 58 years old and alone.

"By the way, I'm Andy, Andrew Fannon to be exact."

I don't know how much you know about Houston Texas, but it's known for its heat and high humidity. The summers can be scorching, hot and steamy. We have mild winters most years, but it can hit below freezing sometimes.

Heck, it even snowed in south Texas when I was a kid on Lincoln's birthday, if you can believe that. I remember running outside to feel the icy coldness of the snow. It was beautiful falling from the sky. Why most people in south Texas have never even seen snow. It was amazing and for it to have fallen on a school holiday was almost unbelievable. Sort of like the Lord must have decided to grant someone's dying wish or something. I'll never forget that snowfall and how it felt.

Of course, since then, I've seen lots of snow all over the world. But the first is always the best, especially if you are a child. During my tour in the Navy, and through two marriages, I've visited all sorts of places. I've been to most countries in the world at some time or other - Most states in the US too. This is one of the fortunate items in my life. Traveling throughout the world has always been a high point. I've seen lots of things and been to lots of places.

I guess I kind of drifted back to the past there. As I told you, I'm kind of a history buff and I believe our past helps shape our present and future. It's all one big journey.

I need an escape from the RV I've been living in, so I decide to drive down the block to my new local hangout. I'm in the middle of my second divorce and wondering what the world holds next. If I could've only known, I might've stayed on that bar stool. My world is about to turn upside down in ways that I can't even imagine.

"The real world is stranger than fiction" they say.

Anyway, getting back to my delightful Single Malt Scotch, (the reason I'm careful to call it by its name, is there's a big difference in Scotch or "Malt Whiskey" to the Scot's), I sip away, delighting in the warmth of it,

THE WHITE SUIT

smoothly rolling down my throat. Is there anything in this world more comforting than a good aged Single Malt Scotch? I don't think so. I'm trying to forget my present situation and the Scotch is definitely helping.

After my first wife Kate got so controlling, I found myself on my way out of the marriage - it was really a case of self-preservation. Otherwise I was on my way to disappearing, disappearing from Andrew Fannon into Kate Fannon's lackey. Scary thought. The song *Staying Alive* comes to mind for some strange reason. *Hah!* I can picture John Travolta dancing away, throwing that arm up in the air. *Hah! "Staying Alive, Staying Alive.*

I was diminishing on a daily basis, by the time I found the courage to leave. Ever felt that you were disappearing? Slowly shrinking into oblivion? Well, I finally decided to cut my losses and run before I totally disappeared. *Hah!* That's a good choice. I don't miss the fighting, nagging and bossing around. And I found Andrew Fannon again! *Nice to see you again Andy!*

That's when I meet Vicky again. I say again, because she was an old schoolmate of mine from military school. Vicky was an upper classman that I had ogled over. I thought she was *wonderful* - fun to be around, *the life of the party*. We were on the golf team together, but she would only date upper classman, and rank meant a lot in military school. She was out of reach in those days.

The military school I attended was co-educational - so there were girls there. Most military schools around the country were male only. This particular school was different. Most of the students were from other countries, mostly Saudi Arabia and Venezuela. Their parents worked for oil companies overseas and sent their children to boarding schools. Also a large number of students were *Trust Fund Babies*. In other words they were rich kids put in boarding schools so their parents didn't have to raise them. Most having family Trusts (or Old Money) that paid them lots of money, essentially never having to even think about having a job or worry about money. They couldn't ever spend all of that money and many tried very hard to see if they could. I didn't really understand what a *Trust Fund Baby* was at the time. I did learn just what this meant shortly thereafter though.

Meeting Vicky again at a class reunion is refreshing and exhilarating. Such a change from the life I'm presently living. She's vibrant, full of life, laughing, talking and loving. At least that's how it looked on the outside. I have no idea that inside, Vicky is living a life of torment - torment that will lead her into medication after medication after medication. You see, I will finally give up on my second wife of nine years, Vicky. After dealing with her self-absorbed hypochondria that resulted in a multitude of doctors,

THE WHITE SUIT

medications, and continuing stupors, I've finally lost hope.

"Rehab?" you ask?

"Sure I tried that, a couple of times actually."

But every time, Vicky slid right back into her *doped up stupor* - oh, it takes a few months, but it's always the same. Gradually finding new doctors to prescribe new medications for every ailment she thinks she has. Migraine headaches, stomachaches, IBS, incontinence, bladder problems, high blood pressure, kidney problems, muscle problems, shoulder problems which include a bone spur, sinus, respiratory problems, Bell's Palsy, mini strokes, heart problems, Essential Tremors and the list goes on and on. And one medication's side effects just lead to another ailment. The list is endless. It just gets to be too much, I mean like 19 medications per day, multiple times daily. Can you imagine the chemical reactions going on inside of her? She's to the point now, that she sleeps all day and stays up all night, the TV on 24/7 and she hardly ever leaves the bed. She has two maids and a cook that essentially take care of her.

Vicky doesn't drive so at least three days a week she forces herself to get up and one of the maids drives her to the *Dr du jour* for new prescriptions or to renew the ones she already has. It's a pretty pathetic life and unfortunately there's not a thing I can do to help her. As a child, Vicky had once walked in on her Dad engaged in a gay love tryst. And, apparently Vicky had two abortions which she claimed were miscarriages. I found out about these long after I married her, from one of her good friends, very late in the marriage. She had a hysterectomy at age 22, maybe as a result of the abortions being botched. I guess these memories manifested all at once. Medications alone were costing about $1500 a month – so unable to help her, off I went. Hindsight is always 20/20. I wish I'd known earlier about all these things.

Why is all this happening to me? Am I a jerk or just a fool?

Divorce lawyer in hand, I'm set for a fight, a real ugly, doped-up fight. Now I'm dealing with lawyers. If you've ever been through a divorce, you already know the scene, it's ugly. Lawyers love to keep the war going, that way they stay on the payroll. They stretch it out for as long as possible to line their greedy little pockets.

I moved out of a beautiful house and am now living in a fifth wheel RV that I own. Enough room for a single guy, but not luxury accommodations for sure. If you're unfamiliar with a fifth wheel, it contains the bedroom overtop of the arm-like area that hitches into the bed of a truck. Mine has three slide outs, one in the bedroom, one in the dinette area and one in the entertainment area. It's quite roomy and has all the things I need, but I do miss the old house.

THE WHITE SUIT

The house that Vicky and I shared, sat on a cliff overlooking a large lake in south Texas. Even though the lake has gone down in level, it's a beautiful house with a beautiful view. Much time has been spent renovating the house so that it's just the way we like it. I have so many personal items in that house. Things gathered on exotic trips, things left to me from my family, things that I've built. I miss the maids and the cooks. It was a life of luxury. I didn't have to lift a finger. Everything was done for me - laundry, cleaning, cooking. I have my own workshop at the old house. It's full of tools and is suited perfectly for my hobbies. I love making things. Now I'm on my own, doing all these things for myself. It's quite a change. I used to sit out on the porch there, watching the lake, puffing my cigar and sipping a Scotch or Malt Whiskey. But at least now I don't have to deal with Vicky.

Oh yeah, I'm still at the bar, and some commotion is snapping me back. I guess I'm sitting here thinking over my past - funny how your mind drifts sometimes.

The front door has swung open and a burst of cool air makes me shiver - out of my side view, a young couple comes into the bar and slides onto two barstools a few seats down from me. I size them up a little but don't pay too much attention. The male is somewhat overweight, not obese, but definitely chunky. They're in their twenties. The gal is attractive. They're blabbering about it being their first date. They seem happy to be with one another and are conversing very easily.

Down the bar from them, a gal is playing a video slots game. She's an attractive Latin Anglo woman. It's about nine o'clock at night and I remember wondering why such an attractive gal is in a bar alone playing machines.

You see, here in Texas, video slots, commonly known as "eight liners" are legal, but not legal. They're legal if they don't pay you actual money. Therefore, you'll find these video gaming devices in many, many bars. However, some bars do pay you money. It's done *under the table* and very quietly. This is not legal. But it's quite common and the authorities don't seem to have the time or resources to correct the situation. This is one of those bars. They pay the winnings, *under the table*.

Pretty typical day at the bar, not real crowded or exciting, but it's conveniently located around the block from my RV. And it's a nice warm place to smoke my cigar and not feel too lonely. Being surrounded by just a few people, even people I don't know, is better than sitting alone at my RV. And it's not easy to find a place willing to accept cigar smoke. Times are changing and it's hard to even find a place to smoke a cigarette let alone a cigar. I find most establishments have signs up reading "no cigar smoking". I love the smell of a good cigar and really can't figure out why other people don't enjoy the same aroma.

If you think about the quality of air, well heck, you suck in more fumes going to work on the freeway than you would ever get from breathing in someone's smoke from a cigar. And it would be so much more toxic - diesel fumes, gasoline emissions, factory smoke. Who in the world is worried about a little cigar smoke compared to the toxic fumes we breathe in everyday, running everyday errands. In my opinion, these people would profit more from trying to clean up the freeway air. That's just my opinion of course. *Hah!*

I took another puff from my cigar. The smoke is slowly escaping and filling the bar with an aroma straight from Cuba, there's nothing like one of those cigars. I smuggled a couple into the country when returning from Costa Rica last year – I only try to smoke them on special occasions. *I guess this qualifies, divorce number two. What a dreadful thought.*

I haven't had good relationships with women. My life seems to fail with women. First there was Kate, now Vicky. I don't know if I'm picking the wrong women or if I'm just unlucky at love. *An even worse thought is that it could be me. Am I poison to women? Do I turn them into mean, dysfunctional beings?* Either way, these two women have taken a lot from my life, both in assets and in emotional turmoil. One I lost because of her controlling ways, the other due to her anxiety issues. Both seemed to come from very dysfunctional homes. Both were abused in some way. *Was I trying to rescue women instead of marrying women for true love?* Marriage and love are illusive to me at this point. I thought that I loved them when I married them. They seemed perfect at the time. Things all went well for a certain time period, but once things went wrong - they really went wrong in a big way.

"Do I have any regrets?" you ask.

"Nah, not really."

As I'm thinking over all these things, conversation at the bar is getting a little loud. That couple that came in earlier - it seems the guy is bragging on being a Navy Seal and about all his endeavors. He's getting quite loud about it, seemingly to impress his lady friend. Bragging that he was in the Navy for only six months but attained the prestigious and grueling qualifications to be a member of the elite Navy Seals, toured in Iraq, was shot at, wounded and is now medically discharged. *Really, all in 6 months time? Boot Camp is 3 months of that - And look at his physique, a little overweight for a fine tuned Navy Seal.*

As it catches my attention, the gal playing the video game approaches him and shakes his hand. She congratulates him on his service and explains her son is also military - Marine. They're talking - but wait - something is going wrong. The video gal looks

THE WHITE SUIT

nervous and is getting increasingly annoyed and loud. She's challenging this man about his honesty. *Is he really a former Navy Seal?* Apparently she doesn't believe him, and quite honestly neither do I.

I've only caught bits and pieces of the conversation, but this man's facts just don't add up. Being former Navy only reinforces this feeling. One of my best friends was former Navy, and he was UDT which is the predecessors of the Seals. One thing about those guys…they don't brag, they don't talk and they never…if ever - reveal they were part of the unit. I don't believe him and neither does the video gal. Ah, our first thing in common, I'm about to meet the next 5 and a half years of my life.

Her name is Caite, how weird is that? She has the same name as my first wife, spelled differently, but pronounced the same.

As the Navy Seal couple slitters out the door in embarrassment, Caite sits down in an empty bar stool close to my own. We start up a conversation about the Navy Seal couple and find that we have chemistry.

She buys me a drink in gratitude for my service, I accept, but, certainly reciprocate. Sure she's a little young for me, (I'm 58 and she's 41) but I like her. She's very attractive, a little heavy in the hips, but that's ok. We talk for quite a long time about her life and mine. She tells me her story of 2 bad divorces, losing her business because of one of her husband's running her into debt. I hear about her alcoholic father and how it's hard to live with them. Her ankle was broken and it incapacitated her for 6 months. She's been trying to live at her sister's house but she has two kids, one with psychological problems. As a result, she finds it easier to live out of her car most times. I find out she's struggling financially and in a lot of other ways so an invitation back to my place flows easily from my mouth. How did that happen - and so fast? I don't know - but it seems so right somehow.

Alright, before you go off thinking I'm some kind of playboy, let me assure you that I'm not. This has nothing to do with sexuality, well almost nothing. I mean, I like her and I could use some love, but not necessarily sex. I'm lonely and have been most of my life in one way or another.

I guess in hindsight, I realize that I must have a rescuer personality. I mean this woman has told me she's in trouble and living in her car. It doesn't faze me; as a matter of fact I think I'm attracted to it. She really needs someone, why not me? I want to be needed; in fact I'm craving it right now. It would feel good to be loved and needed by someone.

I guess if you married your high school sweetheart and were lucky enough to keep a long term marriage alive, this whole story is totally foreign to you. I don't know how to explain a life like I've led. Sure, I've made some bad decisions, but nothing mind altering.

THE WHITE SUIT

My life is calm compared to Paul in the Bible. He was a terrorist that tortured and murdered Christians. He was forgiven and ended up being one of the most well know disciples in the Bible. His writings are extremely important. His life is important. I think that we, who are forgiven the most, love God the most. We understand the bigness of forgiveness. We understand the love of God.

A life like mine is hard to explain to people who have led a more "normal" life. But I believe that God loves us all and uses us in all different ways. So before you go off and get all "judgy" on me, take a breath and remember that not all of us are as lucky as others.

That's why, for Christ's sake, I delight in weaknesses, in insults, in hardships, in persecutions, in difficulties. For when I am weak, then I am strong. 2 Cor. 12:10

Almost instantaneously Caite and I are now a couple. She moves in, we look for apartments, she loses her car, I swoop in to the rescue and we even get a puppy. Her car is old and will cost more to repair than it's worth. I have an extra truck, left from the business. The puppy is a miniature bull dog and we name her *Miss Chesty*. After Lt. Gen. "Chesty" Puller, one of the most decorated Marines of WWII. This is because of Caite's son being in the military - you know - Marine – their mascot.

I'm now an important part of her life, and she's an important part of mine. My divorce now seems less frightening, less important. Love has reappeared in my life. I feel a new happiness, a new hope for the future.

We find a townhouse together, we move in. Things are going along quite well. She has a small business on the side - I have a business left from the divorce (which is still going on). Life is good. I can feel myself being regenerated.

Caite has a large family which is welcome news to me. I regret not having children - my decision seemed right during my first marriage, but now left a hole in my life. She has two children, a teenage daughter and a young adult son who's married and in the Marine Corps. We all take to each other immediately. I love her kids and offer them assistance whenever they need it. She loves her kids, probably too much and we sometimes find ourselves being their enablers.

Wow, life is good. I have an instant family! I'm not sure that I've ever felt like that before. I have a large extended family.

PANIC

The sound of screeching tires! But wait a minute! Things are far from good. I'm embroiled in a bitter divorce and several other legal battles concerning business dealings.

I have a former employee suing me for firing him. Lawsuits like that are so time consuming and expensive. He was a totally useless employee who sat around and did little, went out for breakfast on the company's time, and so many other issues it would be hard to go into here. But I'm being forced to defend my firing of him.

Life is so unfair sometimes. Being a business owner is so unfair sometimes. Small businesses are difficult to keep alive, when things like this happen. Large corporations have large legal teams and they can deal with these petty lawsuits. But we small business owners are hard hit. I think some people make a living by suing people and getting settlements - a new form of welfare.

Remember me telling you about Vicky earlier? Meeting her after my first wife Kate – *the breath of fresh air?* Well, you see Vicky and I lived a very luxurious lifestyle during our marriage. We were rich actually. We had several oil wells and a very successful pest control business. We had maids and cooks, a beautiful house on a cliff and even a guest house. We had clean, pressed sheets every single day, Vicky's choosing of course. We traveled extensively and had acquired many fine things. Vicky was a shopper and we had things stacked up all over the place. Paintings she bought, but never hung (there wasn't enough wall space). Jewelry, of course, was her favorite.

Now that the divorce has hit full swing, Vicky is corrupting not only the funds from those businesses, but also unwittingly destroying those businesses. I had money set aside to repair one of the oil wells and she drained the account. Now that oil well won't get repaired and it won't work properly. In her greedy quest for money, Vicky is draining the funds needed to make the businesses work.

Stress is mounting as well as anger. *How are the two of us going to survive this divorce and have any funds or businesses intact?* It's an improbable outcome. Vicky will be her own worst enemy while trying to destroy me. She will end up destroying the very thing that she needs in order to continue her lifestyle.

THE WHITE SUIT

As we all know, stress can be a killer. And I guess I can attest to that fact. Even though Caite had taken some of the emotional stress away, more came to take its place. There's ever mounting pressure from Vicky and her attorneys. Huge weekly payments declared by the judge. I'm sinking, slowly and painfully sinking. I can't meet all the demands. Vicky's on a quest to destroy, there's no stopping her. *Just how am I going to survive this?* I keep going to court trying desperately to diminish the required payments. They're huge. Everyone wants money; Vicky, my attorney, the court. I have payroll to meet and wells that need repairs.

Biblically it says that our battle is not with flesh and blood, but with spiritual entities, namely, the devil and his angels. That he prowls around like a wolf looking to devour us. It felt like that; that I was being devoured. Sinking, drowning and being swallowed up by something.

These are questions that surround me on a daily basis. I have to say that Vicky sure seems as if an evil presence has taken over her body. Here was the *funny, beautiful, life of the party, golfing buddy*, now trying to <u>kill</u> me both in spirit and financially. How do things go so wrong? What happened to that wonderful *breath of fresh air* that I'd found?

I didn't feel that I had done anything wrong. I didn't cheat on her. I didn't beat or abuse her. Am I perfect? Of course not, but I didn't do anything that would force a person into continued drug abuse. But *poof*! - My original relationship with Vicky has disappeared or rather morphed into some evil, stressful event now threatening to erase my very existence. Do I think Vicky is evil? I don't know, but I do think events happening around me involving Vicky are evil. It at least makes her seem to be evil.

Meanwhile, Caite and I continued our daily life. I have a pest control business, it's doing well. I've pretty much given up on the oil wells and give them over to Vicky. This will make Vicky happy and keep her off my back as well as the fact that they actually belonged to her prior to our marriage in that she owned the corporation. I took the pest control business. After all, Vicky didn't think it mattered as much as the oil wells and she had no idea how to run the pest control company. It didn't seem that important because the price of oil was only $6.87 a barrel in 1998. I mean she couldn't even get a driver's license much less a pest control license, which is required to operate that kind of business in Texas. It's a small business but sufficient to be able to make a living.

Caite continued her little side business. Then as my business grew, Caite joined in, working with me and helping run things. She did some office work to help out and answered routine calls. I had a small group of employees, but did most of the work myself.

THE WHITE SUIT

We're getting along splendidly. Maybe this time I'd be lucky at love. Maybe this time I could finally be happy. I loved the idea of an instant family and Caite being Anglo-Latino, had a large one - parents, aunts, uncles, kids, even grandparents. It felt so good to be accepted as part of a large family. This was something new to me. I'd never had a large family. They're an expressive family too; sometimes there are loud discussions and fighting. But in the end, they all still love each other and large family barbeques become routine. I was the official chef - I deep fried turkeys ran the grill, had crawfish boils, catfish fry's and drank some beer. I suppose at the time, I was so happy to have this "family" that I ignored how dysfunctional they really were. There were alcohol abuse issues strung across generations. I guess I didn't want to see anything wrong. I mostly just didn't want to be alone.

Caite and I had both been through bad divorces with the lawyers and court battles. Neither of us wanted to legally get married again. Now by legal, I mean involving the State of Texas. We were monogamous and felt that we were a married couple. No, we did not get "legally" married. First off, we couldn't until my divorce with Vicky was over, and second of all, we just didn't want the state involved with our personal life. If this had been our first time around, yes we probably would've gotten married in the State of Texas, but since this wasn't the first for us, we felt a marriage by agreement and under the good Lord was enough for us. We acted like any married couple; we just didn't have state documentation. Some people may consider this wrong, but it's what worked for us.

"Remember the RV that I told you about?"

Well, I still own it and went back to work on it one day. The RV had originally been my Houston office. I drove back and forth during the work week to run the pest control business in Houston. I would drive back and forth from south Texas to Houston on Sundays and return on Fridays, living in the RV during the work week. That's a long commute, like around four and a half hours each way. It gets old rather quickly. I began to wonder why I was doing this.

I would return home to Vicky, a drugged up, sickly wife who stayed in bed most of the time. I was there - ended up watching TV mostly. What a life - doctor's appointments three or four days a week and seventeen pills a day. I really feel sorry for her, but can do nothing about it. I tried taking her to rehab a number of times. She seems to be a really tormented person. Have you ever felt lonely even when you are with someone? That describes how I felt with Vicky. She was there, but not there. I did this for about three years before deciding to leave Vicky. Then I lived here alone in the RV for four months before meeting Caite at the bar.

THE WHITE SUIT

Actually I'm working on the truck that's parked here at the RV Park – a work truck. It's early in the morning. I've gotten up before Caite and decided to go work on that truck. I have the hood up, fixing a dead battery. I have all my tools out and arranged orderly on the ground.

It's a cool morning, but beautiful and sunny. The air smells of fresh grass and coffee being made in the park. The smell of bacon and eggs is drifting in the air. Birds are swooping and chattering all around me, the sound of a typical morning in the RV Park. Things are routine and normal. I like the RV Park, it has its own outdoorsy charm, and the people are always friendly at RV Parks, saying "Mornin!" I don't know why, but it's a fact. They seem to all help each other and are basically happy. Maybe they don't feel the pressure of mortgages and lawn maintenance, or maybe it's just the fact that they live so close to the outdoors. I'm not sure what gives magic to RV Parks. I'm thinking about it while hooking up jumper cables to my truck. The cables will run from my H3 Hummer to my truck. The Hummer really looks more like a glorified SUV.

I love my Hummer. It's a dark metallic blue changes color in the sunlight, depending on what angle you look at it - sometimes it turns an aqua blue kind of color. I stopped into a dealership on a whim one day and just bought it. Straight out, just bought it on a whim; drove it out the same day. I thought I deserved it. I was under so much stress that I decided to treat myself to something wild and crazy. Hummers were really cool back then. I guess they quit making them now. Obsolete.

Yes, I'm still here working on the truck back at the RV park.

It's a familiar place – I've lived in that RV for about four months before meeting Caite at the bar. Before that I'd used it for trips to Las Vegas. I liked to play baccarat. I actually got pretty good at the game, made some money at it here and there. My winnings would pay for the trip at least.

Suddenly as I'm working, I hear a *pop*. Not a *pop* in the engine, but from inside me! Somewhere, something has *popped*. *What in the world? What is it?* Suddenly I have a headache, back in the back of my head - down toward the nap of my neck.

I start feeling bad. Something is wrong. I'm dizzy and just not feeling right. My vision seems a little off. *Am I seeing double? I feel like I might throw up.* I drag myself inside the RV.

I lay down on the bed. *Maybe this will pass. Maybe it's just something minor.* I try to fall asleep, but can't. I'm restless. Something or someone is keeping me awake and jumpy. I toss and turn in the bed.

In the New Testament it's recorded that an Angel kicked Paul in his side, to wake him up and help him

THE WHITE SUIT

escape prison. Interesting thought that angels might be *kicking* us to get us to wake up and do something.

I decide to close up the RV and just go home. *Maybe I'll feel better once I'm home and in bed.* The safety of home is suddenly pulling on me. Caite is there and maybe she'll know what to do, maybe she can help me. I need home and Caite.

I close up the RV and start to pull out. Oops, I forgot about my tools and the truck. I reluctantly get out and pull the hood down on the truck. All of these minor things seem difficult now. It took all my strength to pull down that hood. I randomly throw the tools into my Hummer. Do I care if they're all helter-skelter? No, I'm in a hurry! I leave that place in an ever escalating panic. Driving home's difficult. My vision's playing tricks on me. I still feel dizzy. I run red lights when I can - glancing both ways to make sure it's safe. I speed up trying desperately to reach the safety of home. Sure am glad a cop doesn't see me - if I'd gotten stopped and pulled over – I'd probably not be here now telling you about it.

I feel if I can only get home, everything will be ok. I haven't had that feeling since I was a little boy. *Ah, the safety of home.*

The smell of a home cooked meal. My mother wasn't a great cook, but her meals were always good. And the safety of my bedroom at home; I always remember how safe I felt in my room. It was my place

– my kingdom. And my parents were always there to keep me safe.

Oh, what I would give to feel safe at this moment. Oh, to be in the safety of my room in south Texas, with my parents standing guard.

I'm an adult now, I remind myself. *I have to take care of me.* It's a humbling experience to want your mom as an adult. I can't let my thoughts go there. *I must be strong and get to my own home.* They say that "home is where your heart is". I guess that's true. My heart belongs to Caite right now and home feels like wherever Caite is.

Ah ha, I see the townhouse now. But I have to stop at the gate and put in the code. *Drat!* Caite and I live in a gated community. Here in Texas that means a little bit of safety, -makes it harder to come onto the grounds and steal. This safety has now become an obstacle. *Drat!*

This means climbing down, out of the Hummer and putting in a sequence of numbers. Hummers are quite high off the ground - one of the downsides to owning one. The thought of just getting out of the Hummer scares me. *What if I pass out on the ground?* I can't seem to make the number sequence work. The gate won't open. *Dang! Come on!* The safety of home keeps calling me. *Just get home and you will be safe.* After about five failed attempts, the gate opens. *Thank*

THE WHITE SUIT

goodness, I'm now just yards away from home. I made it! - Safety at last!

I clamor into the apartment and race up the stairs. I'm not sure how I did that, feeling the way I did. Maybe fear is creating some adrenaline. My head still hurts. Caite is barely awake, startled by the noise of me taking three steps at a time coming up the stairs.

She jumps out of bed to ask "what's wrong?"

I tell her, "I heard a *pop* and feel really...really bad".

She puts me in bed, gives me five Ibuprofen and I try to relax. *After all, I'm home, someone is taking care of me and it will be ok,* I tell myself. Caite is looking at me with deep concern. Her face tells a story of panic. She's insisting that I see a doctor or go to the ER. I don't want to go, (I don't like doctors) but after much discussion, she finally talks me into seeing her own personal doctor - Caite calls ahead.

You see, my father died before his time, in my opinion. He had cancer. Doctors did their job and treated him. He went into remission. After about two years, his good friend, his doctor, had him do one last bout of chemo - just to be sure the cancer was completely gone. Well, that last bout of chemo did him in. In my opinion, it's what killed him. He trusted his good friend and went ahead with it, even though there were no signs of the cancer returning. Too much of an otherwise good thing, I guess. Chemo even though it's poison, worked the first time and it healed him. That event tainted me toward doctors. They don't have all the answers and they err too much on safety's side. My dad was well and healthy before that last treatment and I watched him deteriorate into frailty, sickness, and then death. He died in 1994. Still makes me mad to this day!

Mom didn't trust doctors either. In the 1950's she went into surgery to investigate a lump and came out with a double mastectomy. She never was the same after that surgery. I was only eight years old at the time. I'd been sent to stay at a friend's house. When I came back home, Mom was in bed and I was told she was sick. It took many years before I knew she had that mastectomy. I didn't find out until she was in a nursing home actually in 2009. But I did know at the time that something bad had happened to Mom. I just didn't know what, but it changed her. Distrust of doctors ran deep in my family.

Caite and I drive to her doctor's office and we are seen immediately. Caite must have told them it's serious. They can't get a good blood pressure reading. They're getting the same look of panic that I saw on Caite's face earlier. My vision's still blurred and I'm seeing double. Seeing double makes me feel nauseous. My blood pressure's off the charts, but then drops down low. It's in stroke ranges, but they can't read it - super high, then almost nothing and then back and forth

THE WHITE SUIT

sporadically. I'm almost in a panic mode by now. *What's going on here?* The doctor wants either an ambulance or Caite to act quickly. Caite decides that she can drive me to the nearest hospital faster than they can call and have an ambulance get to the office.

A feeling of emergency and panic fills the air. Caite's speeding. I'm telling her that I might not make it to the hospital; my disorientation's getting worse. I'm asking God for help.

You see, God and I have conversations. I talk to him on a regular basis. I guess it's part of my inner self. I've always talked to Him in some way or another. It's a natural part of me. I'm asking for reassurance, to calm me. I'm feeling the panic now. *What is wrong with me? Am I going to die today?* My thoughts run amuck. How can I control those thoughts? How can I be calm in a situation like this? *Help me God, help me! Please help me!*

Once we arrive at the hospital, things move quickly. It's the small suburban hospital that's closest to where we live. They're having the same trouble with my blood pressure. They put me in their small ICU. The decision's made to transfer me downtown to a larger, better equipped hospital. We wait an hour for an ICU ambulance. None are available. It takes a special ambulance, equipped with special equipment to transfer an ICU patient. Time is ticking. *Will there be enough time?*

SHANE FLYNN & MADELINE DUFFY

It's funny how slow time moves when we're in a hurry - that slow driver in front of you when you're late for an appointment - those blasted red lights and trains. When we really need to go fast, time slows down. Stress develops this way – our need to control time. In our attempt to get things to go our way, obstacles get in the way, blood pressure rises, our health suffers.

Everlasting life supposedly has no time. God is eternal and we are promised everlasting life. What would it be like to live in a world without time? Is time only a worldly occurrence? I've tried many times to wrap my mind around a world without time – I just don't seem to be able to imagine it. Some people picture us floating around on clouds, just strumming on harps. *Hah!*

I don't believe God would create us for such a dull boring afterlife. There has to be more to it than that, Jesus talks about mansions and golden streets. Now we're talking! I guess I believe in a busy afterlife, with lots of exciting things happening. But I still have a hard time picturing a world without time. Time is so important in the here and now. My personal opinion: time is only relevant to life and death, and otherwise it has little meaning.

The ambulance finally arrives. Time's moving so…so slow. I want it to hurry up so that I can get fixed. My head still hurts. It's an intense pounding feeling. I'm scared. *Don't tell anyone, because it's not*

THE WHITE SUIT

manly for a man to be scared. My military training kicks in and I put up a strong front. *I'm Navy! I'm a man! I'm strong!*

A former Marine is the paramedic in the ambulance. That reassures me somehow. I feel in good hands. We talk about the military. I'm former Navy and Caite's son is a Marine. I relax some. Good people are taking care of me. It feels good. *I'll be ok now. These people know what they're doing.* I try and quiet my thoughts. I know that panic will not help me and it actually may make things worse.

He tells me, "sir, I'll be taking care of you now, nothing's going to happen to you on my watch!" "Usually it's the Navy that's getting us where we're supposed to be, so now it's the Marine's that'll get you where you need to be….just returnin' the favor".

The ride seems to take a long…long time, at least an hour. Houston's known for heavy traffic. It's the fourth largest city in the US. The interstates are good, but there are just a lot of cars and trucks. *Get out of the way people! Can't you see the flashing lights? Move over! I need help!*

Time becomes more important in a crisis situation. Time, time, time……..we are captives of time sometimes. It works against us most often. Not enough time to do this, not enough to do that. Americans seem to be always running, chasing after time. But it escapes more quickly than we can catch it.

Ever slippery and moving onward - like a marching band, marching on and on. *I hate time!*

Once we reach the downtown hospital, things move quickly. I'm admitted to ICU. I give a "Simper Fi" to my Marine Corps Angel. Mission accomplished. People are running around, doing things, and poking me, hooking me up to things. The smell of medicine and disinfectant fills the air. Machines start making noises. I hear a woman moaning down the hall. She lets out a short scream and goes back to moaning.

Caite called her mom while they were transporting me to the larger hospital, and oddly enough, Caite has gone home, her mother picked her up there, they managed to beat the ambulance to the hospital, and are waiting for us when we arrive. That's comforting to say the least. How they drove there that fast in Houston traffic is a miracle in its own. Caite told me later that her mom drove like a maniac and she had her eyes closed most of the time, thinking she was going to be in the hospital with me. Her mom was a little Mexican *Danica Patrick* on the freeway. *Hah!*

A social worker of some kind is assigned to me and asks if I have a Medical Power of Attorney. I know that my soon-to-be ex-wife Vicky holds one for me. This is a bad thought; Vicky with the legal ability to <u>really</u> kill me. She's already been steadily destroying our businesses and now she could actually destroy my body.

THE WHITE SUIT

I tell the social worker, "No."

She asks if I want one and if I do, who I would designate. I designate Caite, my 6 month girlfriend to be my legal, Medical Power of Attorney. A witness is required. Caite's daughter-in-law (the Marine's wife) has arrived at the hospital to support Caite. Paperwork is signed. It's done - Caite now controls my medical destiny.

You see, at this point I'm still very aware of what's going on - sedated, but not in la-la-land. The social worker determines that I'm mentally competent to make my own decisions and legally this will stand up in court. These people have all the training and support necessary to legally support their decisions. I never in my wildest dreams could ever know just how important this decision will be.

Do you ever wonder if God sends certain people in and out of our lives for a reason? Maybe even a very specific reason? I have to say that I now believe this to be the case.

Like the Turkish drafting teacher, what are the chances? It may have saved my life when I was dropped off there in the Navy. And after hating Turkey, I ended up returning there on a cruise with Vicky. I visited Paul's prison cell where he wrote to the Ephesians. It was a spiritual place, peaceful. On that same trip, I sat in an amphitheater where Paul preached. Wild feral cats came to me asking for affection. The tour guide said she had never seen this on her many trips there. She stopped her presentation to comment on it. What this meant, I don't know. There were about 6 or 7 of them walking all over me and purring.

Some people and maybe even animals move in and out of our lives by design. They may not be meant for a lifetime relationship. It may be for just a moment, or maybe for many years. Someday I'll have to ask God that question. It'll be interesting to get the answer. How he decides this and how does he implement it? How does he send these people in and through our lives? There's no such thing as a coincidence in my opinion.

Do angels assist in arranging meetings? Will the next person you bump into in the grocery store, end up having a significant impact on your life? Did an angel cause you to bump into them? All are interesting questions about the supernatural world that seems to surround us. Is there an angel standing right next to you, waiting for you to put them into some type of action? Does speaking out the Word of God cause them to go into action? If I pray for someone, does an angel immediately dispatch to assist in that prayer? Is there an unseen battle going on around us, right under our own noses - just unseen by us because of a hidden frequency or time warp of some kind? Someone or something must have been watching over us all, to not

THE WHITE SUIT

have had accidents or police to interfere or alter our paths with traffic delays or problems. Are angels clearing our paths – probably so; sight unseen, but nonetheless there.

Meanwhile, a neurologist is sent for. Tests are run. Things become foggy for me.

Some things I'm about to tell you are accounts from Caite that I learn later in time, but I'm going to insert them in the right place to keep the story together in a congruent timeframe. Other events are as I remember them, medically they may be out of order or skewed, but this is how I remember them. When you are involved in intense medical emergencies, things can seem different than they actually are.

I'm so happy to have Caite with me, standing by my side, so that she can help make sense of what's going on around me.

I'm in ICU, a peculiar pod of beds arranged in a circular pattern around a nursing station. We are all critical patients, some may not make it. The nurses keep close watch on all of us. I've unknowingly become part of a larger group, a group of very ill people. We're people whose lives now rest in other people's hands and the hands of the Almighty God.

What determines who survives and who moves on, is a question to ponder. Some believe that God causes illness out of punishment or judgment to someone who is deserving of such punishment; Job's friends believed this and told him so. They told him he must have done something wrong, something to offend God. Others believe Satan causes illness just because he's evil and loves to watch pain and suffering. Still others believe Satan causes it and it's up to us whether to accept it or deny it in the name of Jesus, and the power of the Almighty God. It's most certainly a debate amongst many people and spiritual leaders.

Biblically, Jesus healed the sick and raised the dead. When asked why a blind man was blind, and who sinned to make it so, Jesus answered that it wasn't sin but that the blindness was being used to glorify God. Perhaps a demonstration to us dumb humans as to the true ability of the Almighty God. Just how big and how good is your God? Is He big enough and good enough to heal you? Is He big enough to have created you? Is He big enough to raise the dead? Just how big IS _my_ God? The God, who I've believed in since a tiny boy, God, who I talk with on a daily basis, God, who I read about? Did I even have the tiniest bit of knowledge about His true power and goodness?

I know this much; over the course of the next thirty six days I'm going to find out just how big He really is. The following events have enlightened me to come to grasp with so many factions of life, faith, the afterlife, love, hate, technology, medicine, doctors and perhaps anything and everything that one could think of under

THE WHITE SUIT

these circumstances. It's truly a life changing chain of events.

The phrase *life changing* is perhaps overused and underappreciated. I guess you can't fully understand the depth of that phrase until something like this happens to you. It's deep, powerful and difficult. It has the ability to change your mind on things that were solidly instilled previously. I wish I had better words to express the importance of *life changing*. Maybe KAPOW! Something smacks you right between the eyes, you collapse and you arise like a phoenix, transformed. It's an awakening of sorts. *Wake up you stupid human, do you get it yet? Duh!*

They have me on morphine now – I know this much at this time. This is some powerful stuff. Man, talk about la-la-land! No worries, at least on my end of it at this time. But, this will change. The nurses decide when and how much of this addictive drug I receive. *Hey, I'm just like Vicky now, doped up on drugs. Hah!*

I'm plugged into machines; their beeping sound becomes a familiar sound resonating in the background of my new surroundings. Nurses come in and out, prodding me, medicating me, taking care of me.

It's been only about 3 hours since my first headache and popping sound. Time is ticking by slowly, as if in slow motion, yet fast like a *speeding bullet*. One minute you are just fine doing routine things, fixing a dead battery in a truck, the next you are surrounded by nurses and fighting to stay alive.

When the sights, smells and sounds of the hospital get to be overwhelming for me, all I have to do is say that my head hurts, my nurse pushes a button and *BAM* - I go back into la-la-land. It's wonderful at this time. I can escape all the noise, prodding, and fear. La-la-land does have its benefits to me at this time. My nurse is always right here, near enough to talk directly to me. She is so sweet and helpful. I love my nurse Julie.

Man…..this is really some good stuff…..no wonder it's illegal to all but the doctors…

Alive is something we take for granted most days. We go about our routine things, going here and there, not realizing that time in this world is finite. At some point all of our time will run out. It'll be the end of us; auf wiedersehen, arriverderci, adios, au revoir, see ya later alligator.

Or will it?

4

THE FIRST DEATH

The hours in the hospital become days. I feel like I'm in a very small town in far south Texas, in a very small hospital with these circular pods. I'm very familiar with this small town. One of my friends Ned, my Navy buddy, my adopted brother, lived here and I have a couple of oil wells here near Laredo. I visit this small town on a regular basis. It's a one story building, small hole-in-the wall hospital. It's hardly a place to be if you have a serious illness, more of a *cut and scrape* kind of place. I don't know how I got here and I feel as though I've been here a while – I'm tied down and can't leave. Things don't seem right. I'm being ignored. I can't get their attention. I'm thirsty…real thirsty. They won't let me have water.

I fade in and out of our time space. It seems very prolonged. They just ignore any and all of my pleadings. It continues to get worse and worse - *dry, hot, no water*. The nurses are packing things up, clearing out all the pods including all the equipment, computers and all the beds. I'm alone, there are no other patients. Now I'm lying in a solitary bed, no equipment, no nurses. *Where is everyone? Why don't they care about me?* I'm sick and in trouble and they all have packed up and left. Being alone is terrifying.

I'm thirst, so...thirsty. My tongue feels like it's swelling in my mouth. I try and get someone's attention, but there's no one around. I'm having trouble breathing. My tongue is swelling, bigger and bigger; it's cutting off my ability to breathe. *Please someone, bring me water!*

"Water people, I need water," I felt like I was screaming.

I'm getting more and more desperate for a drink. I'm dying of thirst. I feel like I'm in a desert.

"Help me someone, help me. I can't breathe." I'm screaming but my lips aren't moving.

There's no one to hear me. I feel myself slowly gasping and taking my last breath. It's slow, long and final. I remember it very well - that desperate feeling of despair. I feel as though I just don't have the strength or ability to continue on. I feel exhausted and just want to leave here and just go to sleep.

What is it that Jesus told the woman at the well? Ask me for a drink of water and you will never thirst again? That He was the living water?

Wait! I hear helicopter blades whirling. It's a deafening sound. *Whoosh, whoosh, whoosh.* I can hear

THE WHITE SUIT

them but I can't see them. I know from my experience on a naval air craft carrier, that it's the definite sound of a helicopter. I'm looking up, searching for them.

Our helicopters were used for search and rescue. They also transferred supplies from other ships when needed, but their main purpose was search and rescue. I loved my Navy tour on the carrier. I would stand up in the main super structure (the island) and take pictures of all the planes taking off and landing. It was really something - to watch those planes.

If you aren't familiar with the ranks in naval nomenclature, seamen are typical above deck jobs or "rates". The below decks are considered engineering "rates", typically responsible for the mechanical functions required to keep the ship ready and in condition for battle. I was below decks and termed a "Fireman", originally from keeping the boilers fired. My rank was "fireman" but my rate was "Electrician's Mate". I worked in one of the four engine rooms, at the electric switch boards which controlled the electrical distribution for part of the ship and helped maintain the generators and pump motors.

I had grown a long mustache that had handlebars, no beard was allowed for me. This was the Zumwalt days of the Navy. Admiral Elmo Zumwalt was the Chief of Naval Operations (CNO) of the Navy. In other words he was the HMFIC of the Navy. For those of you not familiar with this it means the Head Mother

&*^%#$ In Charge of Uncle Sam's Navy. He helped integrate the US Navy into the modern world of 1970. I was a skinny guy, all 130 pounds of me. Equipment for emergency oxygen (OBA's) had to fit snugly to your face, and a beard would prevent that from happening. The sounds from those planes had affected my hearing. No one wore protective gear covering your ears in those days. We didn't realize that those plane engines could steal much of our hearing. I can still hear, but there's a constant roaring sound in the background much of the time. Small price to pay in the scheme of things....and after all it was service to the country we all love.

I look upward again trying to see the helicopter, but it's not visible. The helicopter has hooked up chains to my hospital pod. I'm not sure if I see chains or just know that the chains are there. I'm being lifted into the air and being transported somewhere. Wow, what an exhilarating feeling, the warm air swirling around me, the feeling of weightlessness and swinging high above the world. The air is warm and comfortable. I'm being swept away to some unknown location. I listen to the steady sound of the chopper blades. *Whoosh, whoosh, whoosh. Someone does care, I'm not alone anymore. But where are they taking me and why? Who's taking me?*

Suddenly I feel my pod descending into a Houston metropolitan hospital. The air stops swirling and it

THE WHITE SUIT

lands with a secure thud. The helicopter sound retreats, then goes away entirely. It's replaced by hospital sounds. Nurses are scurrying around me, hooking me back up to equipment. *I'm safe once again.* I drift back into unconsciousness, feeling secure. I'm not alone anymore. I can breathe but the thirst is still here. I'm baffled and elated by the experience. *I was already in a metropolitan hospital. Why did I feel that I was elsewhere? Why was I transported to somewhere that I already was? What did this mean? This is surreal...*

Caite later tells me that I had cardiac arrest during the night and flat lined. The time was actually 3 am when she got the call. Nurses and doctors resuscitated me. They brought me back from the brink of death - *or search and rescue flew me back* - according to my vision. This is my first near death experience. I died and was rescued by a helicopter.

Am I reading things into a vision? Some people may accuse me of hallucinating on drugs. After all it was really good stuff, but it felt different from that. If it were only the drugs, why would I still remember that vision? Was God communicating with me in some way? Maybe He used familiar objects I had known for rescue. Maybe this is how God communicates with us sometimes, using familiar objects and events? Is He always talking to us in some way? This was not drugs or hallucinations…it was real, I re-live it every time I think about it….it was real.

I think the mundane events of life have a tendency to minimize and drown out God. We eat, sleep, work and play in our own finite reality, sometimes forgetting the very essence of God. He seems insignificant to us sometimes as we deal with the day to day stress of fixing a car, going to work, calling clients and driving in rush hour traffic. *Have we minimized God to the point of extinction or powerlessness? Does He only exist when it's convenient for us? When we finally reach the end of our rope and have no other choice but to rely on Him and his goodness?*

Maybe He was trying to tell me that my care was being improved, upgraded. That He was rescuing me from sub-par care to more sophisticated and life-saving care. I don't have a definitive answer, but I know that I was being rescued from something less to something more and it was supernatural. I remember it today as vividly as I did at the time it occurred.

As time progresses through this, the doctor begins to question Caite's decisions concerning my coma and about being on life support. This is around the time of my first death, several weeks after my admission to the hospital. She reacts to his concern angrily by wanting to know if there's brain activity. He told her there is, but he fears there's probably brain damage. And even if I survive there will be a very long rehabilitation time, and extensive long term care needs to consider. He told her that if she decides not to *turn me off* in the near

THE WHITE SUIT

future, in the case that I didn't improve, that should I survive I would probably do best in a rest home facility for disabled patients and that she should start making plans, but that he didn't have a lot of hope.

She yelled at him to get back with her when there's no brain activity! This thought really scares her. But she prevails and won't even consider this unless my brain ceases to function. She told him if this happens and he can prove to her, that I'm really, truly dead, - ok, but if not, not to bother her again about this - and she stormed out on him, very unhappy. *Thank you Caite, thank you.*

In the hospital, the struggle to give up personal control continues. I'm helpless but don't yet realize it. All the people who surround me - Caite, nurses, doctors, everyone but myself, now have total control of my life. Surrender is becoming easier – I'm tired and broken.

I particularly remember a male nurse giving me a sponge bath. He has a scrubber of some kind on a long handle like a broom handle with a scrub brush on the end of it. He can get to me without getting near me….like I'm something nasty and he can do it from a distance. Truthfully, I don't blame him…I wouldn't want to do his job and I probably am really nasty. I can only imagine. If only I knew….nah I don't want to know. He's flipping me over and using that scrubber as a weapon, scrubbing my most intimate places with a force and vigor that defies compassion. I'm wincing in pain, got tubes coming out of me from everywhere, not a single orifice without one, and where there wasn't one they made one to stick something in. I'm begging him to stop. My intimate areas are stinging from the force of the scrubbing when he finally stops. Not a pleasant experience to say the least. *Surrender to this? Never! I want my life back! Give me my life back!* Ahhh, must be morphine....back to la la land...my head hurts, Julie is there with that magic elixir...ahhhhh. Bless you Julie...bless you.

Other nurses (not Julie) are more compassionate and I wouldn't be telling this story without their careful care. They work a job that many don't appreciate. They are caregivers and life savers. I'm sure that I still don't realize the significance of their work, but I'm thankful for their care. They took care of me when I couldn't. Without them, I would've been helpless and lost. Thank you to all the nurses out there working hard and doing unimaginable things. The human body isn't pretty when it's damaged. Doctors and nurses seem immune to this somehow. They see blood and guts, and don't seem to be affected. Me, I would throw up - the sight of blood makes me nauseous. How they do what they do is a mystery to me. I suppose it's a gift. They have the gift of healing in some way.

ICU nurses have to be the next best thing to angels. The skills and knowledge they possess and practice are

THE WHITE SUIT

unreal. The snap decisions and actions they take every hour of every day mean life or death at any moment. The stress must be incredible. My angel was Julie. Without Julie, Vicky could have tried to sneak in and maybe have turned me off. Julie was the one telling Caite she needed to get my name changed. Julie took care of me – truly seemed like an angel from God. Oh Julie, you truly are a special angel from God, and may He Bless you in all possible ways...Julie, My Angel.

Some of the simplest things, like getting a nice hot shower are out of my reach. I can't go to the bathroom on my own – I'm hooked up to tubes that remove the waste into bags hanging beside my bed. It's a simple existence while other people take care of me. I had taken all these things for granted just a few days ago. They were the everyday chores of life. Now they seem like the everyday pleasures of life.

Isn't it interesting how much we take for granted? They say all things are *relative*. If you're rich, you don't care how much it costs - but if you're poor, the price tag can make some things unobtainable. No one misses anything until it's taken away from them.

I miss my independence and my ability to take care of myself. Other things take on less importance. I find myself missing the most basic things - a shower, a milkshake, my own toilet, a shave, to name just a few - basic things. I'm just beginning to realize, in the fog which has become my life now, the importance of a decision I made upon being admitted here – The Medical Power of Attorney.

5

THE FIGHT

I wake up to a loud banging sound. It's very loud, loud enough to resonate through my entire body. I'm trapped in something small and closed. The combination of the sound and the closed-in-area are enough to really scare me. I'm terrified. *Where is this place?* The only thought that comes to my mind is that *I don't care where it is or what it is, I want out* and I want out badly!

I'm struggling with all the tubes and wires attached to my body. I want to rip them out, get up, put my pants on and go home. Is this the drugs working on my mind? Perhaps it's just human instinct struggling to survive. They have tied my hands down now.

I was told that I actually pulled out the many tubes that were in me – not once – but twice before. This could have really hurt me since I was jerking them out with no assistance or knowledge about the proper way to do this. I could have bled to death. They have to put it all back in again to keep me alive.

A distant male voice tells me to, "Lay still, it will be over shortly."

His voice sounds bored, but it's very loud and echoes. I still struggle. I don't want to be in this terrible place. It's small, noisy and scary, a tunnel of some kind. *Please, please let me out of here!*

The voice echoes again, "Lay still, it will be over shortly."

Turns out they were giving me an MRI. They had to get a good MRI to know my condition and what to do about it. They attempt several. I'm always fighting them, moving and struggling. Finally they sedate me enough to get a good one.

I'm wheeled back to my room drifting in and out of consciousness. Time and people have little meaning to me. My life has become cloudy. I see people, hear people, but don't know what they're doing or really saying. All of these sounds mix together with background noises of beeping equipment, the sound of footsteps, metal clanking, whispering and phones ringing.

The days are starting to melt into one another like one big, giant day. There's little perception of what time it is, what day it is or even what month it is. I don't have my watch on anymore, I don't need it. There's a clock on the wall, but the lights are on 24/7 in ICU. There's no concept of time, and even so it doesn't mean anything, especially when you've been

THE WHITE SUIT

here as long as I have. There are no appointments to keep, no deadlines to meet. Heck, I don't even have underwear on, let alone a watch. I feel naked, stripped of all that's important to me. The light stays on 24/7; no night – no day, just time, nothing more (I understand I was constantly flashing everyone but don't remember it…even my secretary Annie ..oops).

But I keep fighting, *I want to go home.* Home? What's that? I'm not really sure I know anymore, however, it's where I want to be….not here, but there….Home. I even threaten the nurses trying to attain this result.

I tell them, "I'll get that gun out of my pocket and shoot you if you don't give me my pants."

In reality, although I have a concealed carry license, I don't have a real gun in my pants. I rarely carry one with me on my body. Only time I carry one is out in the bush in case I see a snake or some other danger. I guess I thought the threat of one might bring some action.

I want to get up out of this bed. I want to use the bathroom; I want to walk out of here. But no one helps me. I'm helpless yet again. I must just lay here and let other people determine my life and future. I've gone from a man who always worked hard for himself to a man totally reliant on others. It's a humbling experience. An experience that I fight, I want control of myself. I want to determine what happens to me. I want, I want, I want. No one is listening to me or what I want, no one.

My will to fight is getting weaker. I'm slowly resigning myself to the fact that I've lost control, the fact that I might have to surrender, to give up. I don't like that fact. I'm former Navy, self-employed and a self-determined kind of a man. I want control of me. I'm getting tired and exhausted. I want some sleep. Am I sleeping? Things are confusing to me. Time loses meaning again.

Nurses and doctors still come and go - Caite is here daily. Oh how safe I feel when Caite is here. She's my voice. *Thank you Caite for being here!*

I find out later that ICU patients are only allowed visitors for about ten minutes, twice a day and that in order to be in here they have to put on the sterile, disposable gowns, head gear, and shoe covers, the same as used in surgeries. Poor Caite has to do this every time she comes into my room. Upon leaving for a smoke or to eat, she has to take them off and then put on new ones when she returns.

Shortly after I'm admitted, they begin to let her and her only stay with me - as long as she wants. They realize that I'm responding better when she's here, even when I'm in the induced coma. A simple meeting in a bar has turned into a lifesaving encounter - I need Caite.

THE WHITE SUIT

We seem to have needed each other at critical points in our lives. She's homeless after going through a debilitating divorce and on top of that she's recovering from shattering an ankle falling down some stairs six months prior. She lost her business. Even though she keeps going out to her client's homes to do their hair, it's not enough to really live on. Together we solve a lot of problems for each other. I help her financially; she gives me support and new hope.

She's now helping to save my life. Life's a mysterious journey. For me it's more like an amusement park ride right now, a roller coaster crossed with a crazy fun house, and I don't like this ride at all.

Other people visit, but I'm not aware of who has been here and who hasn't. No one seems to matter except Caite. I'm so relieved when she's here. At night she goes home to our townhouse and rests. It must be exhausting for her. She's only known me for 6 months and now is solely responsible for my care and literally my life.

She's taken over the day-to-day running of my pest control business. It's not thriving, but it's holding on. There's no one there to acquire new customers, but it's still running.

Caite's a feisty gal. She's half Latino, half Anglo. She has that beautiful *tanned* look to her skin. Her hair is long and dark. Very independent, she will tell you straight where to go if you cross her. She and her mother have long, loud fights with one another. I guess that's part of that Latino culture. The fighting seems almost like affection between the two of them.

Even though she has so much going for her, Caite's weakness is alcohol. She can drink too much and get mean and crazy. Pain - we all have it in our lives, but Kate's pain is deep. I think that's why she drinks too much sometimes. Well, when I say sometimes, I guess it's quite frequent. I don't want to admit it to myself, because I love Caite. Her family sees it, why can't I see it? But on the other hand looking at her family, she comes from an entire clan of alcohol abusers. I don't want to see it. Caite has become an important part of my life, and I don't want it to end. Just who is rescuing who here? Maybe we both are playing a part in rescuing each other?

Do we all have some type of weakness? I suppose we do. For some people its doughnuts, for others its smoking and for others its gossip. Still others have more severe weaknesses of alcohol or drugs. We all have weakness of some kind. After all, we're human beings - human beings living in a fallen world. I must admit, I do like my Scotch Malt Whiskey, Cuban Cigars, and good cold beer. As Ben Franklin said: "'Beer is proof that God loves us and wants us to be happy."

Now I've met people who think they're perfect. They're self-righteous naysayers that condemn other

THE WHITE SUIT

people. As they stand high on their podium, other people are beneath them, they condemn the weak, little people. I suppose these are the people I like the least in this world. Why doesn't God just slap them across the face to wake them up, put them in their place? Maybe he does and I just don't see it.

Am I doing the same thing as I sit here and think about them? Hmmm, that's something to think about. Do we all condemn in some way and not realize it? Maybe their problem is a weakness too.

In the big scheme of things, I don't know how God even likes us, let alone loves us. Sometimes we do deplorable things. We have deplorable thoughts. How does God get past all of that stuff? Why would He love the human race - baffles me sometimes. I've seen humans be so mean to other human beings - it made my hair stand straight up on my neck - murder, rape, incest. No one wears a sign around their neck that identifies them as a murderer. We have to walk around the earth trying to guess who the bad guys are.

Are we just like a video game - Mario running up and down hills to get power shots. Don't run out of power or you're done for, your Mario will shrivel up and *poof*, disappear. Hurry, jump over that hoop to get more power. Find that key to the mystery box - if you find the key, you will get more power. Fight off the bad guys! *Hah! Sounds like us, doesn't it? Hah!*

Do God and Satan each have a controller of some kind? Are they sitting up on a cloud somewhere frantically moving their joystick? Whooping and hollering as they each win another level? Please tell me this can't be true. I guess I've just reduced the God of the Universe to human level. Yikes, that can't be good. I've actually decided to bring God down to human level, playing a video game. *I told you we have deplorable thoughts. Here's the proof.*

"What is my weakness?" you ask.

"Well, I don't rightly know."

I think it's hard for us to see our own weakness. We are conveniently blind to our own shortcomings. I'm sure I have some, but at the present I can't think of what they are.

"I guess you'll have to decide that for me,

I just don't seem to be able to pin it down."

UNPLUGGED?

The doctors are trying to talk to me. I hear them - I see them, well sort of. They're asking me questions - they want me to make decisions – Caite's helping – she's listening – she's talking to them. They all seem so far away, like in a distant land or something. I'm so relieved to have Caite helping me understand, someone that cares about me. Although our relationship is short, I'm confident in her decisions on my behalf. Caite signs all the necessary paperwork - I trust her.

Caite's my advocate. She's telling the doctors that something more is wrong. I'm not speaking coherently. I'm trying to ask for things but I can't communicate what I want.

"*&%*$%@," is my garble.

I want some underwear and a milkshake! Funny the things we ask for and want at a time like that, simple things. I try talking, but nothing comes out right. Caite's looking at me with confusion. She keeps asking me to repeat myself.

SHANE FLYNN & MADELINE DUFFY

"*&%*$%@," *can't you understand me?* I'm thinking.

It's very frustrating for me and her. My lips are moving, it sounded fine in my head.

I finally ask for a pen and pencil. I try to write out what I want. To me, the writing seems very clear, but in reality it's a bunch of scribbles. Caite saved that piece of paper to show me later. It's a hopeless bunch of scribble - nothing like visible proof or an eye witness to verify the facts. They use that kind of evidence in a court of law; evidence and eye witnesses. Needless to say, I didn't get my underwear or my milkshake. *Chocolate would have been preferable.*

But if Romans 8:28 is true, I guess I'm communicating that there's a big problem here. Caite sees this and continues to fight for me. She keeps telling the doctors over and over again that something more is wrong. This is not my normal self.

The doctor finally listens to Caite - now the doctor is explaining to me that he's going to do an Endovascular Coiling. A cable will be inserted through my groin and make its way up into the back of my head. It will have a coil on the end of it. He's going to have a look see.

He's about to explore my brain. The doctor wants permission to do what he sees fit once arriving at my brain destination. The neurosurgeon is my primary provider. His explanation of procedures, of which there

THE WHITE SUIT

are several options, is that he's first going to attempt this Endovascular coiling, if that doesn't accomplish what he wants - then he'll immediately do an open brain procedure, where he cuts out a big part of my skull, exposing the brain and physically remove the blood clot or the aneurysm itself. It's all very dangerous and risky.

Ah the brain, a largely unexplored part of medicine. The brain holds mysteries that medical science has only begun to explore.

A number of scenarios are described, and the clincher is that he'll leave me semi-conscious so that he can talk to me during the procedure. I didn't care. I just wanted him to fix me.

Fix me doc. Fix this so I can go home. Give me back my life. Sure, it's not perfect. I'm embroiled in a heated second divorce, a couple of lawsuits and my life is stressful. But it's my life after all, all that I have. I'm trying to cope with the hand I've been dealt. I'm a survivor.

And I'm squeezing out any little bit of happiness that I can find, Caite being my newest little bit. I feel that she really cares for me. We both have been through struggles, but we've found each other and are trying to build something. It's working so far. We like each other.

Oh how I wish that I was back in that little hole-in-the-wall bar sipping on a good Single Malt Scotch and puffing on a good Cuban cigar. Yes, that would be very nice right now - yep that would be nice.

The doctor's talking to me once again. He says he has good news and bad news. Surprise, surprise, surprise. Ever heard that before? It seems that the bad news is, the Endovascular coiling shows I have a brain aneurism, the good news is - no repair is needed – I'm healing myself. He's actually quite amazed as well as puzzled. I guess that little coil on the end of that cable could have sealed off any bleeding, if they found a rupture, but all he saw was a healing blood vessel.

He said that I needed more time to heal. The doctor is amazed - You see 85% of the people that have brain aneurysms never make it to the hospital. There's a miracle taking place here. Medical science can't fully explain it. They know what's happened but don't understand how I survived it.

The doctor can't even explain why I seem to be healing on my own. He wants to do this Endovascular coiling again in a few days to verify what's happening. It's a relief to finally know what's happening but the final outcome is still unknown. My life's still in jeopardy.

Medical science only has so many answers they can provide. Mine is a work in progress. The good Lord would decide my final outcome. And I say *good*, because I believe that God is *good*, inherently *good*. He's all that you could ever want in a supernatural,

THE WHITE SUIT

eternal Father. He looks after me with a love that I can't fully understand.

Do I deserve Him as a father? - Not likely. Oh I try to be a good guy. Actually I'm a pretty good guy. I don't murder, steal, or rob. But I realize that I'm good mostly for my own selfish benefit. I don't murder anyone - I don't go to death row. I don't steal because I really don't want to end up in an eight foot by eight foot cell for years of my life. I guess I consider the Ten Commandments guidelines. If you want to live a good - full life - listen to the rules.

As a society, we all have rules; don't speed, clean up after yourself, love your family. The reason we have rules is to keep the society functioning in an orderly fashion. It makes our life good. If you throw out all the rules, life will be chaotic and crazy. Rules are good in most cases.

Although as human beings, we do get off track once in a while. We can overdo rules, we can underuse rules. But I guess if you follow God's rules, things should turn out ok. I guess it's like a roadmap to me. Follow God's advice, his direction....it should lead to a good place. *Right?*

Everything rested in His hands now, not the doctors or my own.

I don't think I was cognizant enough to thank God at that time. Biblically it says that we should give thanks in all things. *Really?* Should I be giving thanks that my head *popped* and I was helpless in a hospital?

Many people have interesting theories about this *giving thanks thing*. That having a flat tire, late at night, in the rain on the freeway should be a time of giving thanks. After all, maybe that flat tire is a gift from God, keeping us from a fatal accident, a mile down the road. That maybe an angel caused that flat tire, just at the right time and in the right place to keep us safe. And what about those people that were late for work on nine eleven? Were angels putting obstacles in their way to make them late?

I guess as a Christian I believe that guardian angels are watching over me and helping protect me. At least at some level I believe it. But do I REALLY believe it? Really, truly believe that I'm surrounded by invisible beings working on my behalf? I do at some level, but I'm not sure that my mind is fully capable of taking it all in. When I close my eyes and try and picture it, I come up short. I do actually know that I'm very thankful for being alive. Little did I know or realize that the *pop* in my head would lead to this.

Whoa…I am really very thankful to be here, even under these circumstances. I'm alive!

Meanwhile my almost-ex-wife Vicky has discovered that I'm in the hospital. She starts calling the hospital every ten minutes. Many times she's connected to the ICU Unit only to be denied

THE WHITE SUIT

information since she's *estranged* and Caite has the Medical Power of Attorney. This aggravates Vicky even more. The nurses have more important things to do than talk to Vicky.

Caite made the nurses aware of the situation prior to Vicky's attempts. Since Caite's here almost continuously, every day, she and the nurses all became friends. The nurses actually like getting this information as it helps them become more personal and understand the circumstances that probably caused me to be here in the first place - sort of like a medical history or background.

Vicky is gathering her "team of lawyers". Vicky sees an opportunity to end this divorce early and not have to divide any assets, but she needs more information which she can't seem to get.

Vicky does not drive, so she relies on the phone for information. She sends her best friend Shelly for a visual report. Shelly shows up at the hospital wanting her youngest son (my Godson) to take over my pest control business. Vicky wants this to happen. He's nineteen and just barely out of high school. Vicky conveys this to Shelly, so Shelly's right there as quickly as possible to try and accomplish this. They want control of the bank accounts. My situation gives Vicky an opportune moment she wants desperately to take advantage of.

Shelly shows up at the hospital in her full grandeur. She's a striking woman and gets attention everywhere she goes. She's about five foot seven inches tall and very, very slim with long, waist length, auburn hair, and a loud mouth. She *floats* into the hospital in her full length, dark mink coat, long auburn pony tail, and red tennis shoes – demanding to see me and wanting answers. Remember earlier my discussion about "Trust Fund Babies?" Meet Shelly.

What a piece of work. I've known Shelly since Vicky and I dated. Her life in some aspects is quite tragic. She grew up wealthy, and she and Vicky have known each other since they were five. Briefly, her father was a flamboyant Texas real estate promoter and developer. He was a major alcoholic and died at a young age of a massive heart attack. Shelly was just out of high school and married her boyfriend, the son of a politician. In less than 6 years she went through over 150 million dollars in inheritance and is now divorced and financially strapped. Shelly's relatives are also Trust Fund Babies,

Ok, well, I learned to understand this Trust Fund Baby concept because I've meet some of them. Even though Vicky grew up wealthy, she isn't a Trust Fund Baby, but this is the crowd she's hung with her entire life. She's a "wannabe Trust Fund Baby" and thought that I could develop her into that same kind of wealth and we did live a very lavish lifestyle after making

THE WHITE SUIT

some good investments. I don't know if I can explain how brutal this type of person is in their quest for money, it becomes their life's blood.

Well, imagine how this goes over with Caite. She reluctantly allows them into see me for five minutes, then realizes what they're up to, and has them removed. This does not go over well as you can imagine - Caite is livid. Now Caite knows about the divorce and how heated it's become. I shared all of my information with Caite prior to this event, and she also knows who Shelly is and my Godson. Our lives are now intertwined. She's fighting Shelly. Shelly's son could potentially ruin my business. He's a young inexperienced boy that knows nothing about the pest control business and holds no licenses. He doesn't know a roach from a June bug.

Vicky is calling my secretary at work, digging for any tiny bit of information as to my condition and how it can be used against me. But my staff is loyal, and they refuse to give her any information.

My secretary, or maybe I should call her my assistant, since she accomplishes so many multiple tasks in the office, knows Vicky. Her name is Annie and she has been with me for about four years at this point. Annie doesn't like Vicky or Shelly; she sees them for what they are. Vicky is enlisting her best friend Shelly to call. I guess she thinks they might give Shelly information that they have been denying her.

You'd just love Annie. She's an African American lady, grew up in the Wards of Houston. She's "street smart" and a real scrapper. You don't want to make her mad. She and I are only 3 days apart in age. She and I hit it off from the moment she came to work for me. We have a very special relationship and a tremendous respect for each other. She always has my back. You couldn't ask for a better friend, much less such a devoted employee. Nothing is going to slide by her...no sir...nothing.

Fight them Caite, fight them. Fight them Annie, fight them.

Vicky's threatening the hospital with lawyers saying she has Medical Power of Attorney and that I should be unplugged - that she knew that I wouldn't want to live this way. That she's still my wife, and that her opinion should be heard and acted on.

Caite's fighting her. I can't fight, my condition is just too debilitating. I can't speak or write. Caite has to be my voice. Caite is fighting.

Vicky calls the hospital continually, over and over again, threatening law suits.

The hospital realizing that Caite has the newest Medical Power of Attorney, changes my name on the hospital records and admits me under an alias, Vicky can't find me that way. The hospital is fighting for me too. I'm too ill to fight. Ah, the power and importance of that document, The Medical Power of Attorney.

THE WHITE SUIT

Hello, my new name is Jackson Ford. This becomes confusing to me as nurses come in, read my chart and they call me Mr. Ford. *Who is Mr. Ford?* Caite keeps telling me about the alias, but it's hard for me to remember. I've lost more control, even my name. *But, I'm Andrew Fannon!* No, you're Jackson Ford now. Andrew Fannon is now in hiding - hiding from my evil soon-to-be ex-wife Vicky. *Hah!*

Do you believe in demon possession? Are there demons roaming around the world just looking for an opportunity, a weakness, an open door into our soul? Do they jump inside our bodies and take over our lives?

Certainly C.S. Lewis brought them up in the *Screwtape Letters*. It's a diary of letters written from a senior demon to a lesser demon trying to secure the damnation of a Brit named only as "The Patient". Whether C.S. Lewis actually believed in demons or not, I'm unsure. I've not read the book in its entirety, but maybe I should put this on my list of things to finish. I think I quit reading it because I don't much care for reading about the dark side. I really prefer reading about good things, helpful things.

Are there hideous little creatures looking for a victim? I'm not sure how I view this side of the spiritual realm. Certainly the idea of gross little creatures lurking about the world sounds very farfetched to me. The movie *Gremlins* comes to mind - those ugly little things causing mischief and misfortune.

Can such a spiritual being exist? Are they fallen angels turned Gremlins?

Biblically, demon possession is noted many times. Jesus Christ cast them out and threw them into pigs. I guess they need some place to go - and they're so dumb as to run over a cliff and drown. I have a hard time wrapping my head around this one. But since I believe the Bible, (it has been on the best seller list for a long, long time) I believe it must exist. Jesus said so and he did something about it. So it must be true - perhaps more of that spiritual plane that I spoke of earlier?

One of my favorite shows is Star Trek. I love the adventure and imagination of the show - strange worlds, strange beings with strange powers. The show takes your mind, firmly planted in our own world, and transports it to a mystical world. The fact that it's actually shown on the screen in front of me helps my mind go there. I don't have to just imagine it - there it is in full color, on my TV. In Star Trek, good always wins. It's a battle of good vs. evil and good always triumphs. I like that part a lot.

I also like *The Matrix*. The idea that an imaginary world could exist within a real world is really cool. The heroes have to plug into machines to transport them out of this fake world into the real world of alien beings. Granted the real world in *The Matrix* is very dark and evil. But what if the real world was bright and good? Do we just need to "plug into" God to see the real supernatural world?

All of these images kind of merge for me somehow when it comes to my belief system. There has to be something out there, something bigger than ourselves. I certainly don't believe that a random big explosion caused our creation. I do know that for a fact. It makes me laugh sometimes to think how some people can believe we all came into existence from one *Big Bang*. The random nature of the theory is just so…so random! *Hah!*

What if there's this invisible world running parallel to our own? A spiritual world of some kind, that we have trouble seeing or even imagining? Some people witness that they've caught a glimpse of that world. People see angels, hear God's voice and even have near death experiences.

What if certain words spoken can call that world into action? The Bible talks about that world a lot. Jacob wrestles with an angel all night - fallen angels mating with the daughters of men - God speaking light into the world, and breathing life into man. And then there's Jonah being swallowed by a whale. I Googled that question once - just to see if it had ever happened in real life - a man being swallowed by a whale - it surprised me to find real occurrences of men being swallowed by fish. I guess it's not as impossible as I first thought.

SHANE FLYNN & MADELINE DUFFY

The questions of the universe surround me. I have to decide for myself what I think and what I believe. I've found through all my years, that this thinking and believing system changes somewhat. I wouldn't say that it changes my fundamental belief in God the creator, but rather reinforces my belief in God. Perhaps I'm ever learning and discovering new things and seeing more proof of His existence. I do believe that we exist in a multidimensional world – somewhere that a physical and spiritual plane intersects - perhaps a parallel universe consisting of angels and our own physical bodies, coexisting in the same space.

What if you took the Bible and put it into a movie in today's world? You know, brought it up to date in the present. Would anyone believe it and go see the film? I've seen the 'Ten Commandments' with its epic performances and special effects. It seems like ancient history. The Red Sea parting and all; but what if you transported it into today's happenings? It would be an interesting project; maybe Jacob's ladder would be "Beam me up Scottie". Would it make it more believable? Would Trekkies now be Christies? That's a cool thought; Christies; everyone dressing up like Jesus with robes and staffs, performing miracles. Isn't it funny how we seem to worship things like *creatures from another world*; dressing up like them, talking like them, trading cards and pictures of them; yet when it comes to the miracles of God, we hide them. We

THE WHITE SUIT

promote the miracles of Star Trek and hide the miracles of God. What would the world be like if we discovered how to heal the sick and cast out demons like Christ did?

"Wow," is all I can say, "wow."

Can we tap or plug into that power? His disciples did, they performed miracles of healing the sick and casting out demons. Maybe we could clear out our mental hospitals in one fell swoop. *POW!* Wouldn't that be neat - send in a bunch of Christies to clear out our hospitals. After all, the Catholic Church still performs exorcisms. Now there's a movie waiting to happen. I would be the first in line to buy the first ticket! *Hey Stephen, Stephen Spielberg, I have an idea for you!*

I feel like my life's a movie right now. Vicky is the big ugly Gremlin trying to pull out the plug. Caite is the little furry Gizmo trying to save me. Life is stranger than fiction sometimes. Or is it the other way around - my life is the fiction, like in *The Matrix*? Maybe this is all one big nightmare and I'm going to wake up. Wake up in a sweat, wondering how I could have dreamt such a thing. I'm actually craving for that to be true. *I'm asleep and I'm going to wake up. Wake up Andy, wake up. Life is normal, there's no emergency.*

I was put into an induced coma to give me time to heal. Time, names, people just disappeared and went away. I was sleeping, a deep, deep sleep.

THE CHOICE

Click, click, click. I'm walking down that long, white hallway. I'm walking toward a distant light. The floor appears to be very large white tiles of some kind. And when I say large, I mean four to five foot tiles. The hallway is luminous white and appears to be lit from some outside light source, but there's no outside light source - kind of like white clouds are lit up, but not fluffy. There are no windows of any kind. The walls and ceiling are a glossy white solid surface. Nothing is really sparkly like glitter, but rather just lit up somehow. Maybe like a light box looks, light coming from the inside, sort of behind the walls, rather than the outside. Maybe luminescent is a better word. Whatever it is, it's magnificent and totally beautiful. It was by no means a blinding light, but rather an engulfing light. It's all around me, surrounding me and keeping me warm and safe, a feeling like a nice warm blanket on a cold night.

The light I'm walking toward isn't real far away, but still distant. It seems like a block or two away. I can see its beautiful glow. It's very inviting and warm. It's a brilliant white light and the hallway disappears into this light - a doorway or an entrance to something or somewhere. I've heard that white light is the presence of all colors, and it felt that way, like the presence of all things. The light that I'm heading toward seems to be the source of the hallway light.

I'm finding it hard to describe, it's so unreal and nothing like you would find on this earth. How do you explain an experience like this? Magical, supernatural - words just aren't enough.

Click, click, click. I'm still walking toward that warm white light. I feel that it's the direction for me to go. It's not pulling me, but I'm moving toward it. Forward I go, *click, click, click.*

The warm brilliant white light is my destination. I don't question the destination. I just know that's where I'm going, meant to go and destined to go. It seems good, a good place to go. I have no hesitation at all. I keep moving forward at a steady pace.

I don't remember being given a choice at this point – it's just a place I'm headed for. *Am I dead? Am I in Heaven?* Thoughts like this cross my mind, but in a distant way. They don't seem to be important or meaningful questions. I can't say that I question much of anything that is happening to me. It's all complete

THE WHITE SUIT

and all ok. Actually better than ok, it's wonderful. That feeling engulfs and surrounds me, a feeling of everything being just as it should be.

My surroundings are warm, comforting and safe. I'm not afraid. Actually it's probably the opposite of fear, I'm happy to be here. There's no other sound except for the clicking of my heels on a hard white surface, maybe from a hard marble type floor. It reminds me of the sound of military boots marching. In military school we would put metal taps on our heels to create that sound. *Click, click, click*. I like the sound. It's strong and steady - neither fast, nor slow, just steady.

I don't remember any smells. No aroma of water mist or hot cookies coming from the oven. This is something that did not exist in my experience. No smells whatsoever.

The light seems to be a commonality with other people's near death experiences. But this is not a dream, but a real experience with feelings and comfort, yet mysterious, but very, very real. Only in experiencing it can one fully appreciate the reality of it. If I could only get that one point across, I would be very happy. It's not a dream, it's real! I think this the hardest part to communicate, the realness of it.

People want to explain away things they don't understand. They want to put it into categories of something physical and real in this world. Like maybe it's the drugs or the brain malfunctioning – but how do we explain the supernatural? I'm not crazy or hallucinating, this is real. I know that for sure deep in my soul, but how do I tell you that? I'm not sure I can, you will have to decide for yourself. I can only tell you what I experienced. I can only be a witness.

As I'm walking down the hall, I'm not conscious of having any clothes on in particular. I mean, I do realize that I have shoes on because I can hear them clicking. But I didn't look down at my shoes. And if you think about it, the last time I saw myself, I was lying in a hospital bed with no underwear, only a hospital gown flashing the world most of the time. I definitely didn't have any shoes on; I was barefooted most of the time. They were actually trying to keep the room cold for sterile reasons. Sometimes they'd give me socks, but never shoes.

About halfway down the hallway a very large mirror suddenly appears on the wall to my left. It took up most of the wall, floor to ceiling, ten to fifteen feet long. I'm intrigued so I turn to my left to look in the mirror. It seems very unusual to find this mirror in this particular hallway, somewhat out of place. It confuses me and startles me a little, but I still feel compelled to turn and look. There's no threat to my safety in any way. It just feels natural and the thing to do.

I see myself, as I am at that time. Fifty eight years old, a gray beard and mustache, but dressed in a solid

THE WHITE SUIT

white suit. I have a white cotton shirt, white silk tie, white patent leather shoes, white socks, and a tailored white suit, totally and completely white. It's a nicely tailored suit, it fits me perfectly. I've never actually owned a white suit, except for a rental tux that I wore to a wedding once. But this is not a tux, rather like a great fitting Armani suit. I've owned all types of suits in my lifetime, everything from custom tailored to Armani, so I know what a good suit feels like and how it fits. This one qualifies in every aspect, it's an awesome suit, fitting perfectly, and very comfortable. It was single breasted with three buttons. The center button was fastened, just the way I would wear a good suit. I actually look quite dapper. I like the look. It feels good. I feel like Ricardo Montalbán in *Fantasy Island*. Mr. Roarke. *Dah plane, dah plane! Hah!*

Now that I think about it, this is part of the reason I feel so comfortable and safe. I'm dressed in clothes that fit me perfectly, look perfect and are buttoned exactly the way I like it. I understand the comfort a little more. Things are just the way I like them - perfect in all aspects. Comfort in its ultimate, along with style and class. Yep, this is an awesome look. I now see that this event has been designed uniquely and specifically for me, Andrew Fannon. It's personal and comfortable for me – just me alone. I'm special and someone or something has taken great care to make this event a one of a kind, an Andrew Fannon kind. Wow, how cool is that? *Hah!*

Perhaps this explains why each near death experience is different. They're never meant to be the same, but an individual experience, each giving a different glimpse into the afterlife.

My skin tone is still flesh and blood - I don't look ghostly or anything. I do look well rested and clean. I look exactly like Andrew Fannon looking rather clean, pressed, and well dressed. I'm well groomed for a fancy occasion. That's the feeling – dressed for an important event.

I wouldn't call myself handsome or anything. But I'm not a *schlock* either. I'm not a tall person; I stand about five foot ten inches in real life. I'm neither thin nor overweight. Sure I have a little spare tire from drinking an occasional beer, but nothing extraordinary. I'm a pretty average fellow I guess. My mother always thought I was handsome. And I always looked great in uniform. Now I seem to have a different uniform, a white suit. And it's nice. I look great! *Hah!*

As I stood looking into the mirror, in my beautifully tailored white suit, I hear a voice somewhere inside of me. It's not an outward voice, but rather in inner voice of some kind. People talk a lot about ESP, and I guess that's what it is. It's more of a thought than a voice, but I definitely know what the thought is. The meaning is totally clear to me. I can

THE WHITE SUIT

hear it, but not with my physical ears. It's in English, my natural language, or is it? Does the language matter? Is it even a voice? Regardless, I completely know what it's saying or thinking. It's a deep comforting feeling. There's no fear or threat at all - only total comfort and total calm. Peaceful and loving might better describe it. Loving, yep, that's the feeling.

But I know instinctively that it's an important event, life changing. I'm not sure how I know that, but I do – the importance of it all. It's very, very important! Very!

This voice or thought is giving me a choice – it's asking me a question.

Do I want to continue on toward the warm white light or turn around and go back to the world? I have to contemplate this question as I gaze into the mirror. The white light is very enticing, warm and beautiful. I know in my heart that it would be a good choice to go forward and into the light, but should I choose it? It feels like a short time gazing into that mirror yet there's no time limit, no rush, because I knew exactly what I should do. I knew my choice instinctively - it's something from inside of me. I don't know how to explain it exactly, I just know. It feels like unfinished business in my gut.

At this same time I remember thinking about Caite and how hard she's fighting for me. And I remember Vicky and how hard she's fighting against me. Do I abandon Caite and the fight with Vicky in favor of the warm peaceful light? This is the contemplation going on in my mind right now. I'm still gazing into the mirror and thinking.

This is a tough decision. I know somewhere deep in my heart and soul that either decision would be just fine. There's no right or wrong, just different outcomes, like a fork in the road. Each fork takes you to a different destination, either will be ok. Sure it would be an escape for me, from the stress of the real world, but it didn't feel that way. I didn't feel any condemnation at all for either choice. Either would be a good choice. There's no feeling of guilt or escape. I

THE WHITE SUIT

could just *check out*, but that didn't even enter my mind. I could escape all the stress in life and trade it in for the entrance into the white light. You would think that this choice would be appealing - to escape stress, but it's not a factor. I'm not thinking of escape, but rather one of duty.

Something inside me doesn't want to give up. I don't want to leave Caite struggling against Vicky and I really don't want Vicky to win. I don't want Vicky to be able to unplug me.

Evil like that should never win. It just isn't right. Good should always win the fight!

Without moving my lips or speaking with my tongue, I somehow communicate with the voice. I decide to return and fight. Vicky will not unplug me! That would be a hideous way to leave this world, being unplugged by your vicious soon-to-be ex-wife. I would be leaving Caite alone. She would feel deserted and that I had abandoned her. We're just getting started - it had only been 6 months. I couldn't do that to Caite. She'd been fighting so hard for me. I must go back and see this thing through to the end. I feel it deep inside, the feeling of wanting to go back. I must go back. I have to finish this thing. *I must go back.*

I turn to my left and take a few steps back toward the left. I hear my heels click again, click, click, click. Nothing forced me or pulled me to turn, it just seemed right and natural. It was my choice and I made it. No one talked me into it, or tried to convince me. It was a choice that I made by myself, about myself.

Instantaneously I'm returned to my hospital bed. I'm still in the induced coma, I think. Time seems meaningless in the scheme of things, but I do remember things seem to speed up upon my return and things started happening, physical things in the world as we know it. The nurses are weaning me off morphine, trying to feed me, wanting me to take pills.

I didn't tell anyone what just happened to me. I'm not sure why, but it didn't seem important at the time. So many things were happening around me that it just melted into the background somehow. It just didn't seem important to anyone except me at the time.

Maybe the shock of coming back into reality is more powerful at the moment. And it's a shock to come back. The shock is a startling kind of effect. Sort of like a dream and waking up, but not really. It was more like you had just gone on a trip of some sort and were now back at work. The vacation takes a second seat to the work. Yes, that's more the way it feels. Like returning from vacation and the shock of having to go back to work and dive right back into the projects you left behind - something like that, only amplified times 100. *Hah!*

Another thought on this is that it was suppressed by supernatural means – that I'm not supposed to remember it at this time. That it's something that has

THE WHITE SUIT

its own season and is waiting to be revealed at the right time, at the right place and for the right reasons. I think this has more validity and is the more definite answer although supernatural is so hard to explain or determine. God is mysterious and has His own reasons and timing for everything.

"Challenges?" you ask. "Yep," Caite has many challenges throughout my tenure in the hospital. Not only is she there every day, all day, and half the night – she's fighting Vicky's continuous pressure from the attorneys (four of them – I guess it was Vicky's *staff* of attorneys) trying to take over the Medical Power of Attorney, the business, the bank account, my vehicles, dealing with the doctors, determining my life or death, among a few.

I have a banker friend and my attorney helping Caite at this time. They are good friends and give good advice to Caite. Luckily they had met Caite prior to my hospitalization and felt comfortable letting her decide things. They knew that I trusted Caite.

Thank God once again for Caite – I really can't imagine anyone but her taking care of my welfare – no one else I've known or do know would have that kind of strength, stamina, or stubbornness. She wasn't letting go of me.

As I improve, feeding is another attempt at futility. I guess the heavy morphine influence on my body makes food taste horrible - all of it. It doesn't matter what they bring, it all tastes exactly the same. *Yuk!* It is a very heavy medicinal or maybe metal taste, I'll never forget it. I could however drink a partial can of Ensure. Caite brings that into the hospital, since the hospital won't provide it - my only nourishment except for IVs. I still want water, but still can't have any.

You see, unknown to me, I have a severe sodium deficiency and water will strip sodium from your body. I sure wish someone would have told me – I might not feel so desperately thirsty. Caite is giving me ice chips along with the nurses. It helps but never seems to fully quench the thirst, and I'm consciously unaware of the ice chips.

They're asking me to report additional headaches. The doctor does another Endovascular coiling. The reports are the same, I'm self-healing. The doctor finds this incredible and very strange, he's puzzled. He's relying on protocols due to the nature of the illness. The protocol calls for one more Endovascular coiling to complete the sequence, yet to come. Frankly, I think he's so confused by the events unfolding that he has to rely on *protocols*. There's no scientific, medical explanation for some of the events transpiring here.

At almost every funeral I've been to in my life, I hear, "The good Lord giveth, and the good Lord taketh away."

THE WHITE SUIT

I've now come to find out that God did not say that. It was Job that said that and God instantly corrected him. My God is a <u>good</u> God. He would only take away something that was going to hurt me. Like a father wouldn't ever let his toddler play with a loaded gun. But as an adult, that same father may teach his son how to use a loaded gun in a proper and safe way. Guns aren't bad - people under the influence of evil are bad. People aren't bad - but evil influence is bad. God tells us that our battle is not with flesh and blood, but with evil forces.

"Know your enemy," is what I say.

It's the fundamental knowledge of every battle - *know your enemy.* There's my military training coming out. *Hah!*

Now I begin to want normal life things. Things like a real shower and a shave. I'm itchy and feeling rather gross. It has been many, many days since I'd had a real shower. I beg my nurse Julie for a shave. She tells me they're not supposed to do that. I beg some more and lovely Julie relents and gives me a partial shave. You see I have a beard and mustache, but only a partial beard. Julie shaves my cheek and neck areas. Oh how good that feels. Thank you Julie, sometimes the smallest things give comfort. You're a doll Julie!

I'm rapidly recovering. My voice comes back. My ability to communicate comes back. They begin to wean me off the morphine. Gradually they start removing the tubes - one now, another later, and so on, until I'm finally free of them. The one down my throat is the worst. It seems to be at least ten feet long. I don't know how they got it in there and actually don't want to know. Hope I don't ever have to endure that again. Same goes for the catheter – now that one will get your attention! *Hah!*

Things are greatly improving – I'm becoming cognizant of my situation. I'm actually gaining some strength. I am however, becoming extremely annoyed by that guy they call the 'Respiratory Therapist'. Poor guy, I actually feel sorry for him as they're probably the most despised person we encounter. Anyone having encounters with them will know what I'm talking about. But, he's here, and he's very persistent. After a few days of him torturing me every few hours with that giant tube they make you blow into for what seems like hours, I notice him observing the main machine that I'm hooked up to. I ask him what he's watching and why. He points at a number and says he'll go away and leave me alone if I can make it to ninety. It's around seventy at the time. He said that it's a blood/oxygen ratio, and that ninety is his goal. Again I wish I had known – I would have tried harder. As soon as I learn this, I hit ninety very soon after. My Respiratory Therapist is now gone. *Hah!*

THE WHITE SUIT

I also learn about my problems with all of the various oxygen masks they tried to use on me earlier. I have a vague unpleasant remembrance of this. It seems they tried all of the types that they make on me and I would fight their use on every one of them. It was the same problem I had with the MRI they told me – claustrophobia. I guess my oxygen level was declining to the point where they were fearful I might develop pneumonia, and they didn't want that. A lot of people develop this condition when hospitalized and that is the actual cause of death, not the original condition they were admitted for. I find out from Caite, that during that time when I was writing all the gibberish and trying to talk and couldn't that I actually had a stroke, that was later proven by that MRI just prior to the endovascular coiling procedure.

Things are rapidly improving to the point that they begin to consider moving me out of ICU.

I move to a semi-private room. I have a roommate. We don't talk much; he's in a lot of pain. Ironically, he's a former Navy officer and has a back and kidney problem - he's about to have a spinal tap. A nice guy, a few years younger than me, in the same boat I guess, no pun intended. Other people are trying to fix him while he relies on their expertise and care. We don't get much time to talk – we're both busy trying to heal in one way or another. People and nurses keep us both occupied doing other things - always poking you with something sharp all day and all night. *I wonder what happened to him.*

I'm sitting in my bed once I was moved to the room from ICU. I am informed by my nurse that the doctor has released me and I am being discharged. I think this is the happiest moment of my life. I'm discharged from the hospital. But Caite isn't here. I need to let her know, but I don't have a phone. My nurse graciously offers me hers and I call Caite. She's home and asleep and I wake her up. She thinks it's the hospital with bad news again since she doesn't recognize the number. I tell her the good news and guess what? She doesn't believe a word I'm saying, she just thinks I'm lying to her to try and escape again.

It seems that I attempted to do this numerous times while in ICU which is why they had to restrain me in the bed. They had my hands and feet tied to the rails with gauze. Quite creative actually, I could just barely reach each hand enough that I could mess with the knots, but there was no way for me to get them untied. Evidently I amused Julie with all my efforts and promising to be a "good boy" if she would just let me out of them. When that wouldn't work, I'd threaten her with my gun again that was supposed to be in the pocket of my jeans which were lying on the floor …just out of reach. What a joke!

Well, Caite doesn't believe me at this most crucial point. What am I going to do to convince her she needs

THE WHITE SUIT

to come get me out of here? Just about that time my nurse comes in and I tell Caite that she's right here and needs to talk to her. She tells Caite who she is and yes, I'm free! Caite tells me that she'll be there but it'll probably be about an hour and a half by the time she showers and drives to the hospital. That was the longest 90 minutes. Time moving slowly again…

Here, four days ago I was in ICU and now after thirty six days Caite comes to take me out of that hospital in a wheelchair, which they tell me is mandatory till I clear the door. So they wheel me down the halls, down the elevators and as we get about twenty five feet from the door I stop them. Under much protest they stop. I get up and literally walk unassisted out of that hospital to the car….everyone is shocked and Caite is pitching a fit….but I'm walking out of that place and no one is going to stop me…I'm free!

I find out from Caite as she begins to tell me her story of what actually happened that the chain of events I've just described occurred over a very short period of time. It seems that at the time I was given the choice, I had flat lined about 3 am in the morning (don't know what it is about that 3 am thing again, but?). They called in the "crash cart" or whatever, and started trying to revive me. They worked on me for about five minutes before successfully reviving me. They called

Caite at the same time telling her I had "crashed" and they were working on me but that she should get there as fast as possible because I might not make it. From that moment of revival or my return from the "white hall", two days lapsed before they transferred me to the semi-private room, and I was out of ICU. That's how fast my healing took. It was exponentially happening …from dead to miraculously healed. Two days elapse in the regular hospital room until I walk out of that hospital.

I walk out of the hospital with no permanent side effects. I have a floppy right foot for about a month afterward, it's quite annoying, but it returns to normal after a few weeks. It kind of flops when I walk and looks a little strange as I walk along - I feel a little like a circus clown, with one big shoe on one foot. *Hah! Bozo lives again!* Clowns have always kind of scared me. Clown humor escapes me somehow.

Caite and I return to the townhouse. Things begin to return to some kind of normal. Had all this been one big bad dream? I know it's real, but since this was the first time I'd ever been hospitalized for anything, it seems surreal on some days. Other days it feels like a big chunk of my life had just disappeared, not to be reclaimed. I feel lucky to be out of there, don't get me wrong. I can now go back to my normal life. Wow, let me think about that for a minute.

THE WHITE SUIT

My normal life is in chaos. I'm still embroiled in many legal proceedings and I bet my company has suffered in my absence. I'm now being faced with *catching up*. You know the feeling, when you come back from vacation, and you need a vacation to catch up from the vacation. *Hah!*

I put it all out of my mind for the time being. I'm just glad to be out of the hospital and going home. I'll just have to face one obstacle at a time, and it feels good to go home. This will have to be enough for right now, this minute. I'll just have to face the other things as they come along. And guess what? I finally got my milkshake, chocolate of course! *Hah!*

I discover that I just don't care about some things anymore. The urgency and priority is changed. Events that distressed me in the past seem to calm down somehow. I don't care about the pest control business anymore. Vicky and her lawyers don't mentally bother me as much. A certain *peace* is flowing over my life. All the issues about work and divorce seem like junk, a kind of junk that I don't care about anymore. Fighting and winning take a second seat in my life.

I'm advised by the doctors that the chances of another reoccurrence are about ninety nine point nine percent to one that it will ever occur again in my lifetime. All told, I was in the ICU unit of the hospital for thirty six days, walked out totally healed with no medication prescribed, not even an aspirin. Don't take any prescribed medication besides an occasional over the counter, even to this day.

The doctor could only say, "Isn't the human body a miracle?"

BEFORE AND AFTER

Here I sit, admiring a beautiful sunset on the lake, north of Houston, sipping a fine old Single Malt Scotch Whiskey and smoking a good cigar, contemplating the last six years. You see, my aneurism was in February 2008. I realize that God wasn't ready for me yet and I must have something much more important to do for Him. What that is, I don't know exactly, but there must be a purpose I haven't seen yet. The question, *why*, of course is always here. Perhaps I'll never know - yet again perhaps it's to tell this story so that it might help bring someone else to Him.

It actually took me a few months to tell Caite about my near death experiences. I'm not sure why it took me so long, God's timing I guess. It seems that as we discussed all of this over a period of weeks - after getting out of the hospital things would start coming to me about the events. These aren't things that are readily available in my mind that just pop out, these are deeply rooted things that as I began to hear the stories, events in my mind would surface and I could recall them and talk about them. Things begin to make sense. When these events surface they are very detailed and parallel the actual events so close that I know I wasn't dreaming them. They are all correlated accordingly. She is very interested and tells everyone about them. Caite was the biggest advertisement for recounting my experience. The events of this were so powerful that it also helped her understand just exactly what I went through and what amazes her is that as I shared this with relatives and friends the story never changes and is almost a word for word story of my walk down that white hall.

Aneurisms are strange beasts; Deadly. Eighty-five percent of the people that have one never make it to the hospital, with most dying instantly. I truly feel that I could've been one of them. The fact that I survived is truly a miracle, especially considering I don't take any regular medication, and haven't since my release from the hospital. Oh I might take an aspirin now and again, or maybe a decongestant, but nothing regular.

Let me continue with events that transpired once I left the hospital. Some of those times I'll never forget.

To begin with, shortly after my release from the hospital which was on a Tuesday, I'm notified by my attorney that I have to be in court on Friday for a competency hearing. This court is about four hours away in south Texas and I have to appear at 9:00am

THE WHITE SUIT

Friday morning. So on Thursday, Caite and I will have to drive to south Texas and spend the night in order to be in court Friday morning.

You see, Vicky and her staff of attorneys are unaware of my release from the hospital so they decide that while I'm still there that they will try to seize the pest control business and remove anyone they deemed "undesirable" from having any access to it and more importantly seize the bank account. They're attempting to have the judge rule me incompetent and appoint Vicky as guardian of me as well as all assets.

Well, I surprised the *Hell* out of them - I lived! *Hah! Triple Hah!*

I don't call them in advance - I just show up at that court hearing. I wish you could have seen the look on everyone's face as I (a dead man) walk into the court room totally on my own and alone - just me and my attorney. Vicky was stunned! *Hah!* Oh the look on her face was priceless! *Hah! Hah! Hah!*

What a great ending to a terrible ordeal! As I'm laughing to myself inside, it suddenly becomes a moot point as they scramble to save face before the judge and not look like *the thieves in the night* that they are, in trying to take away everything I have left. To see their face was really worth the drive and strain of only being out of the hospital for two days.

But oh, it's a long and difficult drive. My body is just not fully recovered from my thirty six day ordeal.

Everything hurts a little. I'm kind of sore all over and weak. I feel really, really weak.

But, the immediate battle is over. Vicky loses, or should I say *evil loses*. Sure she'll go on to fight more battles, gaining more assets. In the end, I don't care about the assets. I just want to escape with something that will enable me to go on in life.

My experience walking down that hallway has changed me somehow. Life in this world seems smaller, less important and temporary. All the things that I used to cling to and fight for, now are oddly small. I guess I feel that I have a higher power fighting with me and for me - which He has demonstrated in a huge way that He's on my side.

I received miraculous healing, not only from the aneurysm, but also in my dexterity. Before this event, I found it very difficult to paint or make finely detailed items. My hands would quiver just enough to make it impossible to accomplish. To this day I can create fine detailing without any quiver in my hands. At the present time I can create the most finely detailed and refined items; better than at any time in my life.

The only thing I can tell you for sure is that it changed me. That experience fundamentally changed me deep inside somewhere and gave me a certain kind of peace. I know something now that I didn't know before.

THE WHITE SUIT

As Caite and I discuss this ordeal - that we both went through together - more and more falls into place. After all, thirty six days of a hospital experience can have a tremendous toll on all involved. I discover that all of Caite's uncles came to visit me at some point as I laid there unconscious with tubes coming out of me from everywhere.

One, in particular, Uncle Billy told me that he absolutely never goes to a hospital to visit anyone….period. Well, Uncle Billy came to see me. He said he loved me and he came to say goodbye. He said I looked like a dead person, and he thought it would be the last time he would see me.

On Memorial Day every year there's a huge catfish fry at one of the uncle's lake house. All the family from everywhere comes to it. It's actually more like a family reunion. All the aunts, uncles, cousins, grand babies, and babies all show up for it. It actually is a whole weekend of partying, drinking and eating. This would be the first time I've seen anyone since our ordeal. There's probably close to fifty people there in Uncle Joe's back yard. Caite and I arrive around 11 am and enter the back yard. As we come through the gate and start to make our way in, almost everyone stops talking and looks at us - one of the people there and I'm not sure who, yells out, "here comes the *Miracle Man*", and everyone start to clap. This was very unexpected and actually quite embarrassing. They all made such a fuss and I guess it was at this point - that it all became so real to me...I truly was and am a *miracle man*. From all medical knowledge, I shouldn't be here. Everyone wanted to hear my story. Many of them came by to visit in the hospital, even though I wasn't aware of them being there. They all expected to never see me again. As I told my story to this group and that, it was so clear to me. My story never wavered....not then and not now. It's always the same...verbatim.

Sometime later, one of the uncles who lived in Austin left his home to run an errand. He needed a part for his swimming pool. He left around 10 o'clock that morning to go about five miles down the road to the store. On his way, he had a massive heart attack, veered off the road and T-boned a big tree and was killed instantly. Oddly, it was on Halloween of that year, and most of the family had gathered at the lake again for an event that evening of all the children and grandchildren to safely trick or treat. We got the call around 4 pm that afternoon. Tragic as it was, sometime later, Aunt Betty told me that because of my experience that she was at peace knowing that Uncle Bobby was ok and safe as he walked down that great white hall to be with the Lord. I'm very glad that my experience has been able to help at least one person gain comfort in knowing that where we go is a very special place indeed. I know that it's helped many more than one

THE WHITE SUIT

and for me….that's what it's all about….comfort and peace within us.

Do our soul and spirit reflect more than we know or realize in the world we live in? I have to say that it must. I'm a witness and living proof to it.

When you enter a courtroom, lawyers present evidence and witnesses to prove their case. I'm one of those witnesses. I'm documenting my experience to bear witness. I'm bearing witness to a supernatural world. God does exist! Jesus Christ exists!

And the strange thing about it is - it's easy to get there. The only requirement is to ask Jesus Christ into your heart. You see God is a gentleman and will not force anything on anyone. You have to invite him into your *house,* your body and soul. He will gladly come in, but you must invite Him.

God gave us the gift of *free choice* - otherwise he could have created a bunch of *robots*. He didn't want a bunch of *robots*. God wants *children*. What a wonderful thought - that in the midst of all the imperfect love in this world, you can invite in the most *perfect* fatherly love - One that promises He will never leave you or forsake you - *Perfect*.

I have to say that it confuses me, why people won't take the chance. It's a win-win as far as I'm concerned. I really don't see a downside to inviting Christ into your life. He's a good guy, extending the chance at huge reward - everlasting life. Just what's the downside to that invitation? If we, as Christians are wrong, well there's no big loss - we are just wrong - but if the non-believer is wrong? They have just given up an opportunity for everlasting life. That's a really, really big loss. The giant *Oops* and it will be too late to change that choice at some point.

I say, take the risk. Try it for yourself. Don't believe me, try it out for yourself. It will change your life forever and your death too as a matter of fact. I'm a truthful witness to that end.

Jesus Christ was either the biggest con artist in the entire history of the world, or He's the real deal. Con artists are undoubtedly uncovered and discovered at some point - so I go with the real deal. God's book, the Bible has been the bestselling book of all time. If this was all one big scam, don't you think someone would have exposed it and it would have disappeared?

But instead it's still relevant and millions of people believe it. If millions of people find it to be true, what's stopping you? If you're afraid that you will have to *be good* or *give up your Sundays* and attend church - forget about that. You can take it just as far as you want to and your heart leads you. You can stay home on Sundays and you can't ever be *good enough* to earn your way to heaven. It isn't about *earning your way to heaven* - it's about inviting Jesus, the son of God into your heart. That's the only requirement - Period. Jesus said that there are two commandments that will

THE WHITE SUIT

fulfill them all. One is to love God with all your heart, mind and soul – and the other is to love your neighbor as yourself.

I have friends that had a *heart explosion* when they accepted the invitation; I myself did not have that *explosion.* Each invitation is different and each experience is different. Just as we are all different, so is our awakening and our calling.

We all play different roles in testifying to the reality of God. Believing in the unseen is challenging - no doubt about it - but the rewards are great. Just accept the invitation and go from there. God will give you a path, and it will be your path, not anyone else's. It's a very personal path. It may not be saving the world, it might be reaching only one person; one person that no one else could reach. You see, every single person is important to God - Every single one.

Apparently there are those who feel - *Why would God reveal things to us now that He hasn't already revealed in the Bible?* In other words - He's already revealed all he's going to reveal centuries ago. Are we supposed to think *that's all there is*, and it's up to us to interpret and go from there? That God is asleep and has stopped doing miracles?

The Bible has many mysteries - what we could think of as "coded" messages. Are we to break the code? Upon study of the Book of Revelation, many scholars of The Bible have worked for centuries trying to figure it out and break the codes. Who is correct? How are we to know other than revelations which come to us? Many of these revelations came as dreams and visions - if they aren't shared then what is their purpose - to only save the person that experiences them?

I think perhaps my only reason for my experience is to share it with all that will listen and it's up to the individuals to decide for themselves – I'm only the messenger, not the message. I've actually shared it many times, to many people in conversation. But I think I'm supposed to take it to a larger audience in the form of this book. I want everyone to know what I experienced and to make up their own mind.

My time in the hallway was rather brief. I have no recollection of how long I was there. I have no idea what was at the end of the hall other than a warm, bright, inviting white light. What is past the light, or part of the light, or the meaning of the light was not revealed to me. But I can testify that it's a warm, inviting, gentle place with no threats or anything bad. Yes it's unknown, but when that time comes once again at some point in time, it's as though the 23rd Psalm comes to mind, *"yea, though I walk through the valley of the shadow of death, I shall fear no evil, for thou art with me."* I felt no evil then, and I'll feel and fear no evil in the future. In my heart, I feel it's the entrance to Heaven.

THE WHITE SUIT

My experience only strengthened and gave proof to me that my convictions and beliefs are reinforced and confirmed, and removes that *blind faith* aspect of being a Believer. There no longer is that blind faith belief, it's now a real belief...I know, I've seen, I live and have no doubts. There'll be people who believe this story as well as people who don't believe this story. I have no control over this nor do I want control of this. If only one person reads my story and it helps them believe, then my purpose for writing this book has accomplished its purpose.

When the naysayers say that if it's not reported in the Bible, it doesn't exist, think about that for a moment - that would mean that we have put God in small box and that He doesn't perform miracles and wonders anymore. I don't believe that for a minute. God is not small, he's HUGE and currant and relevant in today's world! God is still at work.

Sometimes in conversations with friends or acquaintances concerning this experience I've been asked if I met Jesus or was He there when all of this was occurring. No, I didn't meet Jesus at that time. I didn't have to. I knew His Presence was there. It's just a "given" that I knew He was there and I had no worries. His warmth and love were all around, and since I had given myself to Him long before, it wasn't necessary for Him to be right there at that moment, yet He was there. It might be difficult for others to understand unless you've experienced it yourself. I think that if I would have needed to have Him right there and visible to me at that moment in time, He surely would have been there - more so than just the ability to feel His Presence. Just as it's difficult to understand this phenomenon it's equally difficult to explain it.

I believe God is revealing himself to us daily, moment by moment as He sees fit. This is where I think religion gets in the way of God's message. Religious people want rules and regulations. God is not a message of rules and regulations - He's a message of Love. He loved us so much that he sent His one and only son to die for us. That's Huge!

I have had a few questions about how could I have experienced a Godly afterlife if I was living in sin, since Caite and I weren't married in the State of Texas at the time. People have even pointed out John the Baptist's condemnation of Herod as an example.

As far as Herod and John the Baptist: Yes, that's true about John condemning Herod. But that was under the Jewish Law before Christ's crucifixion. I feel that it's clearly defined in the New Testament that Christ came to fulfill the law and the law was only meant to point out our sin and need for a savior, Jesus Christ.

That once you accept Christ, the law is written on your heart and even though we as Christians try and "be good" and live accordingly, it is impossible in the

THE WHITE SUIT

flesh. That's why we need to be covered with the blood of Jesus. He forgives us past, present and future. That he knows what we're going to do before we do it. I don't believe that you can be in full repentance for all your sinful thoughts and actions 24/7. I believe that once you repent (change your mind) and accept Christ, you are fully forgiven forever. He knew in advance that Peter would deny him three times with cussing and swearing. But he did not condemn Peter for it; he forgave him instead and in advance.

When Christ encountered the woman at the well (5 marriages and presently living with someone), he did not condemn her, but offered himself as living water to her. He told her about her past and present to demonstrate his supernatural ability which testified to him being the Messiah.

I had been through 2 divorces and Caite had also been through 2 terrible divorces and lost a business because of her husband running her into debt. Neither of us wanted to get married under the State of Texas again. We both knew the cost in heartache, court fees, attorney's, etc. Even though we were not married in the State of Texas, we lived a monogamous life as if we were married. I guess we were married under God, just not the State of Texas. I realize that this is controversial in the physical church. I guess personally I believe you can be married under God and not involve the government. I also suppose this is true in many countries around the world.

But most of all I believe it's not your job to judge me, that's up to God. Since this is my real life testimony, I believe God spoke on the subject by taking me to the afterlife where I felt God's presence.

Even though I'm not a father, I can't even imagine my dad sending me to die on some cross for all humanity - No way. But my dad was not God. Good thing, humanity would have just ceased to exist - And my dad was a great guy! What about you? – Could you send your son or daughter to do that? And since Jesus IS God, just in a different body - that means God died for us. He literally jumped in front of the bus and pushed us to safety. How cool is that? - True, unconditional love.

In Acts 2, Peter refers to the prophet Joel and his prophesy that in the end times, God will speak to man in the form of dreams and visions. Now we're talking.' That's what I believe. God talks to us all the time. We just need to tune in and plug in. Hook yourself up to the supernatural God. I have friends who have had supernatural visions. I've read many miraculous stories of healing. I believe these do happen today. I don't think God stopped performing miracles - I think God is still in business. He's in the business of offering you everlasting life through his son Jesus Christ.

THE WHITE SUIT

If I seem desperate to communicate this message, it's because I am desperate. It's so important and life changing. I only hope and pray that I can touch just one single person with my story - maybe that person is you. God has given me a testimony, a witness. As He's my true Father, I hope that I've made him proud. I certainly am thankful for His love and guidance. He has shown me things that He has shown no other. My path is my own - <u>my very own</u>, created specifically <u>just for me</u>.

As for Caite, we lasted five more years. It was a total of five and one half years. It would end badly with her betraying me in love. Caite was an important part of my life and I'll never forget her. I'm grateful for her help in my fight to stay alive. But apparently she was only meant to be a short part of my life and I was only meant to be a short part of hers.

It was hard to give up Caite. I felt that she helped save my life. I loved her family. I felt so indebted to her. But in the end we just weren't meant to be. It took a grueling four months to finally give her up. I finally left the country to try and recover from that loss. And it worked! I got over Caite and have continued on.

I felt I had more to do, more battles to fight. *Where would God lead me next? What battle could I help Him with?* Maybe a victory on earth results in a victory in Heaven. Do the angels cheer and bells ring when we get a victory on earth? Is there a parallel universe that reacts when something good happens here?

I don't know the answers to those questions, but God does. You'll have to decide the answers to those questions on your own. I've had to decide those things for myself. I've been truly blessed in my life, and now, fortunately, I'm with my "soul mate" ...the one that I'm supposed to finish this life with....truly the love of my life... this I truly believe, and may God Bless each and every one of you as he has me.

I hope your journey turns out as special as mine has. Invite Jesus Christ into your life and journey on my friend, journey on! *Hah!* Hope to see you on the other side and we'll take a walk down golden streets together!

The End
&
A New Beginning...

Thank you for reading our book. If you enjoyed it, won't you please take a moment to leave us a review at your favorite retailer?

Thanks! Shane Flynn and Madeline Duffy

"Walk in the light" by Diane Nicholls

A personal note from Shane and Madeline:

As born again Christians, Shane and Madeline both want others to know that God is real. Why risk any other choice? There's no risk to becoming a Christian, but there can be much reward, especially everlasting life after death. If they are wrong, no problem, no penalty. If non-believers are wrong, big "Oops" when they die. Don't take that risk. Everlasting life is a long, long time. Accept Jesus Christ in your heart today. Don't delay or like Andy you may find yourself in a life and death struggle in only a moment. There's absolutely no risk to accepting Jesus Christ as your Lord and Savior, only reward. Accept Him into your heart and feel the explosion. Don't take our word for it, try it for yourself. I guarantee it will change your life forever. It will also change your afterlife forever. Take the plunge. Don't risk saying "I wish I would have, could have, and should have."

If you would like to do additional research, pick up the Bible; turn to the book of John. That is a good place to start on your journey toward everlasting life. Take out no-risk insurance. Take it out now and find out for yourself. You will never be the same. Tap into the supernatural world of the Almighty God. It's quite a journey.

Just say this prayer: Lord, forgive me, I repent of my sins and I want Jesus Christ to come live in my heart forever.

That's it. It's that easy.

May God bless you and keep you.

ABOUT THE AUTHORS

Shane Flynn and Madeline Duffy are co-authors that decided to put Andy's near death experience into writing. As authors, they want the world to know that Andrew Fannon can testify as an eye witness to the existence of the afterlife. The authors, having both experienced supernatural occurrences of their own, that are unexplainable in the world view, can both say that there IS a supernatural world surrounding us.

Just how do you explain the supernatural without sounding like a kook? How do you tell people that a supernatural world really exists? There's great risk in giving testimony to supernatural events. People may label you as crazy or even as a liar. The world does not seem willing to embrace the powerful supernatural world of the Almighty God. But that does not mean it doesn't exist. Whether you believe it or not, it <u>does</u> exist. Your belief or disbelief does not change the reality of its existence, it only affects your ability to tap into it and/or see it. I strongly urge you to tap into it.

Retired from business, they have hobbies ranging from model ship building, painting, traveling and now writing. Both are well educated with multiple college degrees between the two of them. One is Southern born and bred, the other a Yankee. Their varied life experiences combine in a sense of adventure and exploration. Shane's business experience is mainly entrepreneurship; Madeline's is engineering and entrepreneurship. Together they make a remarkable team, complementing each other in most areas of life. They met under compelling circumstances and seemed destined to enjoy a relationship together (another book waiting to happen). God works in the most mysterious ways.

The cover painting, done by Diane Nicholls, titled "The Choice" shows the choice given Andy that fateful day. How would you have chosen? Would you have made the same choice that Andy made?

Since this is a co-authored book that is based on real events, you may find an inter-twining account of events. We have made every effort to be truthful and concise in our reporting of this event. But as in any book, you may find us drifting into philosophical and thought provoking ideas. As co-authors we have found that we agree on many things and we feel this is reflected in our work. Rest assured that Andy Fannon approved this work also.

Shane and Madeline
at Playa Tamarindo, Costa Rica

ABOUT THE ARTIST

The painting was created by Diane Nicholls, an internationally sold artist. She would like to tell you about the painting. She also designed the cover.

The experience I had painting "The Choice" happened during a very profound spiritual time. Andy told me his story about his near death experience. I'd only met Andy once and he described it to me during that meeting, and it continued over the phone and through email. I was very interested in his experience because I believe in the supernatural power of God. I'm a born again Christian and a lot of my work is Christian based.

The version represented was finished after many attempts to show Andy's story in a visual way. Since there are no words in the painting, I wanted to show it in a more visual way. Hence the arrows - Andy didn't see arrows in his experience, but I felt it represented his choice visually.

I struggled with the *all-white* theme that he experienced. I painted it all white at one time, but it just didn't feel that it was totally representative of his experience. Hence the silver blue colors. I felt the color represented a *heavenly type* experience.

Upon completion, and actually all through the process, I sent Andy examples of what I was painting. When it was fully complete, Andy was very happy with the result and said that it felt like I was there with him, experiencing the event firsthand.

Well, an artist can't receive a higher compliment. That's when I knew the painting was finished and complete. After all, Andy was the one who was there.

He really liked the way the arrows showed his experience. The arrow that appears largest, due to it being in the forefront, represents the final decision to return to this world. We both liked the impact of this.

I've come to find out that some Biblical scholars feel that the color blue represents revelation. I found this to be rather interesting and did not find this out until after the painting was finished.

My style is different from the realistic or photographic artist. I like taking on a more graphic approach when looking at the world. My ultimate goal is to give feeling to the painting, making it a living breathing entity all its own - Abstract realism maybe. I think my style fit the experience very well, but you as the viewer will be the final judge of that.

I hope you enjoy my painting. Its original size is 24" x 36" and is composed of acrylic on canvas. If you would like to see more of my work, please visit my website at http://www.artdianenicholls.weebly.com

LINKS

Website: http://www.shaneflynn.com

Like us on Facebook:
http://www.Facebook.com/thewhitesuitbook

Follow us on Twitter: @WhiteSuitBook

Diane Nicholls, Artist:
http://www.artdianenicholls.weebly.com/

Christian Books in Multiple Genres, Join Christian Indie Author ~ Readers Group on Facebook. Opportunities for free books and giveaways.
https://www.facebook.com/groups/291215317668431/

NOTES:

NOTES:

Made in the USA
Coppell, TX
03 October 2022